W9-CFQ-409

agps Marc Angélil, Sarah Graham, Manuel Scholl, Reto Pfenninger, Hanspeter Oester

ANOTHER TAKE

This book explores intersections between architecture and everyday life. It evolved as an experiment aiming to view our work from other perspectives than those expected. It is not a monograph. Instead of presenting buildings as solitary objects, framed by impeccable skies and removed from their messy contexts, we sought out the hidden, informal, ordinary circumstances that accompany the making and the use of architecture.

Short stories were written by several authors from various vantage points; each highlights a fragment of a project, approaches it from a different angle, proposes an alternative take.

An archeological find is discovered on a building site on Lake Zurich. Windows turn into postage stamps. A nature conservation union is propelled fifty years into the future. A castle in the air is sighted above Portland. A child's drawing shows a house without a roof. Newly completed storefronts are left largely unscathed by riots in Los Angeles. A piano in a Zeppelin inspires an airport terminal. A Ponzi scheme thwarts funds promised to a children's museum. A butterfly flutters over an alpine scenery. And the world is glimpsed between strands of silver hair.

The unexpected is encountered at every turn. While buildings are made for specific purposes, are subject to analysis, calculation, and evaluation, de facto human activities can never be fully anticipated. They just happen. And in doing so, they alter the course of design intentions. Herein lies a potential for further discoveries with the capacity to inform the conception and creation of architecture, both formally and informally.

Marc Angélil, Sarah Graham, Manuel Scholl, Reto Pfenninger, Hanspeter Oester

17 Short Stories on Architecture

by Denise Bratton, Verena Doerfler, Claude Enderle,
Benjamin Muschg, Margarete von Lupin

Photographs by Andrea Helbling

Wendy —
For little jumps
and little building —
Sara + Marc

06.24.11

Scheidegger & Spiess

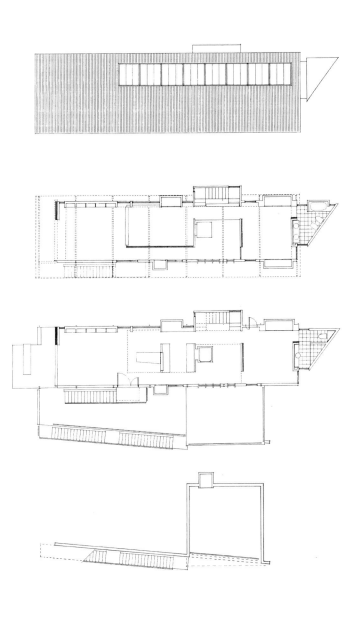

THE HOUSE UNDER THE D

DENISE BRATTON

Like Harold Lloyd enacting his daredevil stunt in the silent film *Safety Last*, the Hollywood House literally hangs out on a limb from its steeply inclined and compressed hillside site. Seemingly suspended beneath the letter D of the HOLLYWOOD sign and the vast wilderness it abuts, the house that Marc Angélil and Sarah Graham built for themselves is nonetheless deceptively secure on its foundations. Less than a year after its completion in 1993, Los Angeles was hit by the Northridge earthquake in the early hours of January 17, 1994, yet the house was undamaged. In a single glance, one takes in the contradictions inherent in a site deemed "unbuildable" before the architects purchased it, as well as the ostensible simplicity of their design for the house. And although it is immediately obvious that they have succeeded in turning every constraint to their advantage, there are a host of backstories that betray the complexity of the process.

In an illuminating conversation, the architects began by talking about the site itself: a little parcel deep inside the canyon where, in the 1920s, developer S. H. Woodruff created the fabled Hollywoodland out

of whole cloth. Their narrative focused on the timeless banner of Tinseltown, the colossal freestanding letters erected in 1923 as a billboard for the housing development on Beachwood Drive. Meant to last about a year, they are still standing nearly a century later, and besides being visible for miles and miles across Los Angeles are familiar nearly everywhere on the planet. The *structure* of the sign intrigued the architects from the moment they started looking at it in relation to the landscape where they intended to build. The casual stance that this anomalous apparatus assumes in a region known for seismic upheaval informed their expressed goals for the house: to think of architecture in a new way, outside the prescriptive restraints attendant on residential architecture in the urban landscape, and to work within a strict economy of means, essentially to erect a house that is as comfortably rooted in its context as the letters of the Hollywood sign.

For this highly idiosyncratic site, with the sign in their rearview mirror, they designed a house that looks like a simple wooden box made of standard-issue two-by-six lumber faced with gray-stained plywood and exposed concrete in the same hue. Defying its narrow footprint with double-height spaces unbroken by interior divisions, the house is grounded deep in an ingenious foundation system devised by Arup engineers, whose principal objective was to stabilize the hill (the house itself is so light that on a level site, it would have needed only negligible footings). In effect, the complexity of the site dictated that this simple box rest on a foundation system so innovative that the Department of Building and Safety considered using it as the scene of a training session for novice building inspectors—a "case study" of sorts. Needless to say, this could have resulted in all manner of delays and permitting miseries, had not officials abandoned the idea once the engineers delivered the special set of plans they had requested as "study guides."

In another contradiction, the simple box of a house is capped, quite literally, by a tensile roofing system—a low-tech version of a high-tech principle—requiring the support of eight tapered steel beams pin-connected into a steel frame embedded in the east wall of the house. Tension cables hold it firmly in balance. Only the continuous clerestory glazing beneath the overhang signals the sheer systemic disconnect between enclosure and roof assembly. This is a complex, hybrid structural system, the kind of technical wizardry in which architects revel. Pitting formal against informal, complexifying the ordinary, and streamlining the complicated, it achieves above all a sophisticated assembly with the humblest and most durable off-the-shelf materials. The trick for the architects was to bring what they had learned (the hard way) about the informality and imprecision of local Californian construction practices into reasonable accord with their own tendency to precision and rationality informed by practice in the Swiss context, where architects oversee the actual building work—in effect, to know when "casual" is good enough, even disarmingly appealing, and when it simply will not do.

The project got off to a start with the purchase of an affordable but admittedly difficult site—not much more than a nondescript "fragment" on the margins of densely built Hollywood, where it disappears into Griffith Park, America's largest interurban wilderness. The site was only affordable because no one else saw how it could be developed. Was it a boon or just a new problem? It was not a matter of either/or, but both, since a new problem is often a boon to inventive thinking, and an affordable lot is only a boon in Los Angeles.

The architects committed up front to engaging all the expertise they did not themselves possess. Their first move was to bring aboard engineers from Arup's Los Angeles office. The plan was to take full advantage of the knowledge pool of an interdisciplinary team, and, out of

respect for the technical difficulties of the site, to prefigure rather than leave matters to chance, finally finding ways to accommodate relaxed local construction standards despite the intent to pursue precision engineering. Typical of their practice, the architects also established from the outset a division of labor between themselves. Angélil was deeply involved in the design and the production of working drawings, but Graham took the lead with this project. Demonstrating a fine instinct for human nature as well as nature itself, she stepped in to make at least two critical moves that guaranteed the project's success.

It was Graham who raised a red flag, sensing that the casual ethos of the construction crew could jeopardize the precision superstructure when it came to tensioning the roof beams. This experimental process had been assiduously mapped by the engineers at Arup, who laid down instructions for a continual, gradual tensioning that would proceed simultaneously across all eight members—like tuning a violin. The scene did not play out exactly as they envisioned, with the construction crew busy looking at their watches and overly eager to "get on with it." Graham called a halt, and assembled all parties on the same spot the next day so that a proper "demonstration" could occur, with the carpenters on one side and the steel fabricators on the other. As the roof assembly was rigged into place, the house finally snapped into focus as a set piece.

Graham was also responsible for determining a truly sustainable approach to the surrounding landscape that ties the house to the wildlands beyond. Stepping back to consider the unadorned box in its rugged chaparral landscape—the habitat of deer, coyote, rabbits, field mice, snakes, and scorpions—the Hollywood House renders the contradiction between culture and nature as palpable as the engineers rendered the tectonic systems efficiently graceful. Her approach to the terraced scape on the north side of the hill that closely hugs the house was to adopt drought-resistant native plants that flourish on the site and act

to preserve the soil from erosion during the infrequent, but sometimes ravaging rainstorms. This was not what her partner had in mind when he advocated a hardscape of gravel—a neutral, low-maintenance approach trumped only by one that requires no maintenance whatsoever, and has eventually come to seem as though it was nature's own doing.

The architects approached the design of the house as an experiment, testing the notion of "house" to its limits. Yet they are unanimous in denying their friend Pierre Koenig's view that the building could be considered a "new Case Study house." To them, the identifying trait of the Case Study houses was *purity* of structure, and not only do they admit to being intrigued by the *impure* construction practices typical of the Wild West, but they also consider themselves intellectually committed to *hybridity*, both in practice and in principle. From the structural point of view, the Hollywood House does indeed play with the possibilities of hybrid systems: the wood construction holds the steel assembly in place. But hybridity requires precision. The rigging of the roof, for example, became an on-the-ground critique of the limits of local building standards, defining the moment when precision was absolutely essential. At the same time, the somewhat hodgepodge handling of certain construction details elicited a new, more tolerant attitude toward perfection than the architects had anticipated. Imperfection was not only tolerated, but viewed with a certain nostalgia for what originally drew them both to the West, with its ad hoc anything-goes *laissez faire*. The balance between precision and imprecision, the letting go of a little "perfectionism" in order to be at home in a new milieu, was all part of the process.

It is tempting to contradict their denial that theirs was a "new Case Study house," if only for the fact that John Entenza's engaging challenge published in the July 1944

issue of *Arts & Architecture* actually made no reference to purity. A commitment to purity of structure may have belonged to the worldview of architects of the time, but in advocating the use of innovative techniques and materials Entenza stressed that "the means and methods must of necessity remain fluid so that the general plan can be accommodated to changing conditions and conceptions." Maybe he was right: the Hollywood House is a new Case Study house after all.

None other than Julius Shulman might have agreed. He certainly approached the house as such when Pierre Koenig sent him over to have a look. Arriving without his camera in hand, Shulman—by then eighty-four but still unparalleled as a photographer of innovative Californian houses—climbed the fifty-three steps leading up the hillside to the front porch. He had made any number of disclaimers on the way up, explaining how he had no time for postmodern architecture—Julius was never one to mince words. To make matters worse, on the day he came to see the house it was in chaos, with painters, drop cloths, and debris everywhere. After some minutes, he retraced his steps, returned to his car, and picked up the camera. Once back on the premises, he began shooting.

Shulman seemed not to have taken in much of the exterior on the way up; at any rate, it was not until the house passed muster that he advised the architects to plant giant agave on the southwestern slope descending alongside the house. Master of scale and *repoussoir*, Shulman was indeed right that "something was needed there." He even offered full-grown specimens from his own densely overgrown yard. When the agave were in and he returned for the final shoot, the house was "styled by Uncle Julius," as he famously used to say. He even coaxed members of the team of architects into assuming the role of action figures in their own production. If one didn't know there was a thriving metropolis less than a mile away, a city of more than seventeen million people, these photographs would make it seem like a house in the country. In fact, the cohesive residential neighborhood that dissolves just past the house where the canyon road dead-ends at the old Hollywoodland Riding Stables is a transitional space between megalopolis and wild landscape, where a local grocery is the social hub, and members of the community share a sense of belonging to the place.

The postwar zeal for home-building, the persistence of the war-born materials that came rushing into builders' hands in the late 1940s and early 1950s, and the love of difficult but extraordinarily scenographic building sites in California are all re-enacted in this project. As a house that accommodates the hard-driven live-work lifestyle of two architects in perpetual motion, it is also very much a product of the late twentieth century milieu, and of a global architectural practice that expertly spans the psychic and physical distance between Zurich and Los Angeles.

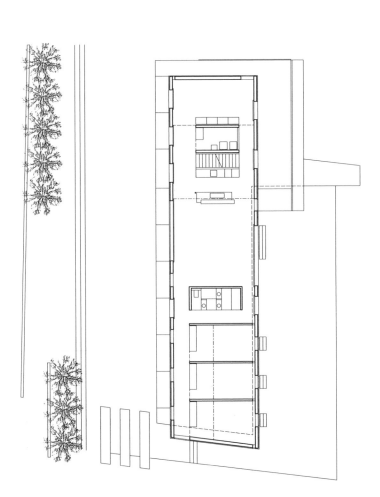

HOUSE WITHOUT A ROOF

BENJAMIN MUSCHG

That a client explicitly asks an architect to design a "living space" rather than a house is no everyday occurrence. The difference is significant, as the architecture envisioned has to be more than just a stage set for the clients' future lives; it has to be a protagonist as well. The consequences of this are far-reaching, as architecture cannot fulfill such a wish with forms and functions, materials and construction, proportions and typologies alone. It has to create space for individual desires, dreams, hopes, fears, and disappointments. The architect is accustomed to slipping into the role of professional layperson, and at that point becomes a complete novice, there being no specialists for the task of designing someone else's life. The success of the venture is predicated on an exceptional level of trust between client and architect. After all, it is still a house that is being built—even if a house without a roof.

In spring 1998, Karin and Patrick Trüb moved into their new home in the town of Horgen, high above Lake Zurich in Switzerland. At the time, Lino, the youngest of their three children, was only a few months old. Four years later the little boy produced a striking picture when asked to draw his house at preschool. Now aged ten, he recalls how "everyone else apart from me painted a house with a roof." Having lived in the house for as long as he can remember, Lino does not regard it as anything special. "There's nothing for you to write about— it's just a wooden house without a roof."

Lino's picture, following the tradition of Synthetic Cubism, combines a floor plan of the whole plot with a street-side elevation, supplemented by numerous *papiers collés*. The large space at the rear with its retaining wall and the elongated building with garage and pedestrian ramp facing the street are both depicted to scale. To the left a lawn or embankment running along the length of the house seems to mark the transition between the street and concrete front yard. But the impression is deceptive, for as with the wooden-slatted facade behind, the elevation is of a vertical lawn growing on the outer wall of the lower house: a wall of earth attached with rebars and jute nets and sprayed with grass seed.

The elevation of the house shows every detail of the cladding of vertical wooden slats as well as the division of the building into three distinct sections. On the left are the three children's bedrooms with floor-to-ceiling windows, and on the right a two-story area with the parents' bedroom and workspace on top and guest rooms below. The central living, cooking, and dining space is sandwiched between the two. Directly above the facade the view of the house abruptly changes back into a floor plan. What looks like strip glazing underneath the roof is actually an elongated skylight that provides light for the large, general-purpose room below the main floor. Lino was consistent in drawing the immense openness of his living space exactly as he so fittingly describes it: as a wooden house without a roof. "Living in this house has changed us," says Karin Trüb ten years on. "Maybe it has made us more receptive to new things." What better compliment could an architect wish to hear?

The exceptional aspect of HT96.4, as this "design for life" is called, is the combination of openness with a functionally hierarchical and rigorously linear structural organization. The parents' realm is at the top of the building, while running below it all along the southern side of the house is the corridor that connects the guest rooms, the kitchen and living area, and the children's bedrooms. All the residential rooms have structural openings connecting them not only to the outside—to the lake on one side and the hill on the other—but to the other rooms as well. The wooden house is essentially a single room packed into a prefabricated wood frame, structured but not divided by gallery floors and shear walls. In this respect the house can certainly be described, and experienced, as a building without corridors, stories, kitchen, or rooms.

"You can feel the weather in the bathroom. It's like taking a shower outside," says Patrick Trüb. The bathrooms form two self-contained islands embedded deep inside the building, top-lit and ventilated by a pivot-hung skylight. The dimensions of the wet rooms adjoining the living area are quite extreme. Although the toilet has limited floor space, its ceiling is about 15 feet high ending with a view of the sky. It is possibly the most spectacular room in the building and certainly a place where one would relish spending a bit of time. The surreal quality of the room is a byproduct of the underlying conception of the Trüb House as contiguous space, rather than as an assortment of stories and rooms, as is the case for most residences.

This packaged space makes no attempt to look like a residence even from the outside. In line with the principle of "form follows law," the building is the maximum size and shape permitted on the plot under building regulations. Resting on the joists of the underground lower house, it is longitudinally and laterally slightly offset in plan and somewhat higher than the level of the front yard. The bulky wooden superstructure does not blend in with its surround-

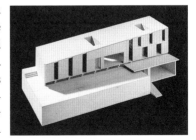

ings, and seems rather to have rolled down Horgen Hill and come to rest by chance on a small ledge notched into the steep slope. The image of the found object, a foreign body in the landscape, is reinforced by the floor-to-ceiling windows on the front and back facades, which create the curious impression that the building lacks scale.

Looking at the tapered shape, the uninitiated do not immediately comprehend what they are seeing. The milkman, for instance, did not offer his services to the family in their first few weeks in the house because he thought the new building must be a movie theater. In fact, the typical scale of a standard residence can be gauged only by the row of windows defining the height of the area below the mezzanine. These windows do give some indication of which stories are where, even if the overlapping systems of roof-high openings and movable sun protection and security screens seems to contradict this impression. While the human dimension is more or less missing from the exterior of HT96.4, it is applied with all the more precision in its interior.

The mezzanine floor divides the space vertically by ending there where ceiling height no longer allows for two stories. It stretches from the western end of the house over its entire breadth as far as the double-height living area, where it is supported at one end and suspended at the other with the result that it looks more like a provisional addition inside a large open space than a permanent fixture. The same principle is repeated on a smaller scale in the three children's bedrooms, all of which are entered under a small mezzanine platform where their occupants will be allowed to sleep once they reach the age of ten. This vantage point offers a good view not only of Lake Zurich, but also of the corridor connecting the rooms. And when the children become more independent, they will be able to enter and leave the house through their own door at the opposite end of the house to the main entrance.

The space for parents and children was kept separate to permit privacy as well as communal living. HT96.4 is a design for life that anticipates the development of a young family without constricting it in any way. The architectural luxury in this house is space, particularly in the high-ceilinged living area, the hub of family life at the center of the house. Yet space is also a key component of the second house underneath.

The dimensions of this lower house, which is made of concrete and can be used independently of the main house, differ from those of a traditional basement. In addition to the garage, there is a single room with 1,400 square feet of space whose 10-foot-high ceiling is supported by concrete beams rather than pillars. Suffused with daylight from a room-long skylight and fully heated, this space is much more than an oversized air-raid shelter and was the core of the building from the earliest planning stages, though not with any specific purpose in mind. It has already functioned as a workshop, laundry room, boathouse, gym, and party venue, and has the potential to be much more. Both the upper and lower houses were designed as open containers, but also as tailor-made living space for a very specific family.

Unless, that is, you change the scale altogether. When Zurich airport's Dock Midfield terminal first opened in 2003, Nora, the family's eldest daughter, was looking out northward from the patio one day when she suddenly pointed to it and said to her mother: "Look, that's our house." From that distance, the 500-foot-long, 66-foot-wide termi-

nal building looks like a 5:1 scale model of the Trübs' family home. The astounding similarities between the two buildings, which were planned simultaneously by agps, throws up a number of questions. Was it coincidence or intentional? Could it really be true that this firm of architects is totally uninterested in architectural form? Might the designers be working on the prototype for a universal building?

While the form of the Horgen residence is an expression of spatial abundance, a design for life that transcends the traditional dimensions of residential space, the airport terminal was shaped by economic considerations. The architects had to find a solution that would accommodate a range of uses requiring different ceiling heights. Arranging these functions under one roof according to height was an obvious way of reducing the amount of land that the building would occupy. It is a perplexing experience for an architect working simultaneously on two projects that have nothing to do with each other to discover that they are increasingly coming to resemble each other.

Preventing the similarity between the two buildings would have meant a great deal of extra work, whereas intentionally helping the coincidence along brought planning synergies into play. Once the initial unease had given way to pragmatic resignation, both buildings were clad in the same vertical wooden slats. They are thus constructed proof of Friedrich Dürrenmatt's dictum: "The more people proceed according to plan, the more effectively they can leave things to chance."

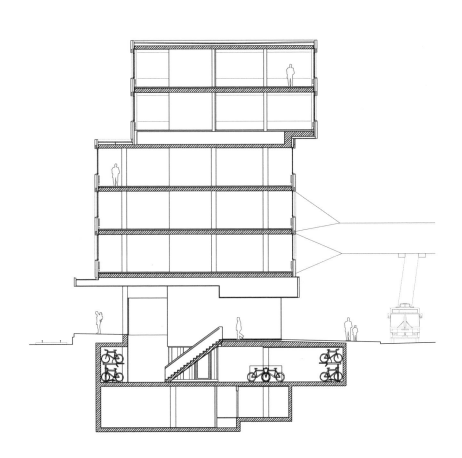

THE MISSING FLOOR

MARGARETE VON LUPIN

It is a rainy Sunday morning and Gisèle Kubourg is drifting through the sleepy streets of Winterthur's old town center. She is planning to surprise everyone back home with breakfast and has decided to pick up a few things at the train station bakery. She crosses the wide Bahnhofstrasse, which for the last 150 years has dreamed of becoming an urban square. Gisèle makes a little game of approaching the station's Renaissance-style portico directly along the center axis so as to keep the entire width of the building in her field of vision for as long as possible—until the edges slip away the closer she gets. Turning right directly in front of the building, she strolls along the facade, and suddenly feels as if she has stepped into the twenty-first century, or at least that is how she would describe it. As she passes the stairs to the pedestrian underpass to the left, she realizes that there is nothing here in these surroundings which appeals to her. Nothing that draws her attention. The asphalt, concrete, glass and stainless steel, the street signs, and bright yellow sheet metal boxes housing the digital displays announcing train departure times are so familiar to her, she no longer registers them at all. It is always the same: trivial and featureless, smoothed by routine, devoid of any enduring meaning. For one brief moment, however, as the sound of cooing pigeons mixes with the thrumming rain and not a single train can be heard, all is still and without any conscious effort on her part, Gisèle suddenly becomes aware of her surroundings.

Walking along under an overhanging roof, Gisèle passes the non-descript windows of a bank. Soon she will reach the convenience store where she intends to do a little shopping. The shop also sells the Sunday newspapers, which are just as indispensable as its fresh bread. She is just about to enter the store when her attention is drawn to a little

red book lying on the curb, all soft and swollen from the rain. She picks it up, brushes off as much of the water as possible, and takes it with her into the shop where she orders an espresso. Walking past the group of taxi drivers busy boring each other with their stories, she takes a seat at the table right at the back, in front of the windows facing the street and dries off the book with a handful of paper napkins.

It takes a while before Gisèle can overcome her slight aversion to this strange and soggy book and carefully peel apart the stuck-together pages. Then, somewhere in the first third, the book at last opens, and Gisèle begins to read:

"What floor did you say?"

Laura Diabolo points at her diagram. "Here, this floor between the first two groups of floors, between the ground floor and the three-story main building."

"Sorry, but it's not on our diagram."

Laura had already heard this answer several times. This visit to the Chief Operating Officer, the head of the real estate and property services company, had been her last hope. It had taken her three days to convince her way past the switchboard operators and assistants and finally arrange a one-on-one meeting—perhaps because of her willingness to pay what could be called a competitive rental rate.

"Mrs. Diabolo, I do admire your perseverance. This is the seventh time that you have visited our offices. I'm sorry to disappoint you, but I can't tell you anything that you don't already know. This floor is not on our list of real estate offerings and cannot be rented. The floor simply does not exist."

"But it's drawn onto this section. And anyway you can clearly see it from the outside. Why else would the projecting roof be so high? And what's the point of building an extra floor if you aren't going to allow anyone to use it?"

Laura should have kept her testy questions to herself, but she was at the end of her strength. Why were they refusing to make floor 1.5 available? She had long since done all the research. The building directly abutted the northeastern set of railway tracks at Vitudurum's main station. Like all of the other buildings close by, it was being marketed under the promising-sounding name of "RailCity." The leasing of existing commercial and office space as well as that of this newly erected building belonged to the railway's newest portfolio management strategy. According to this plan, all large railway stations were to be transformed into busy hot spots and their buildings adapted to house shopping centers and service providers. The entire commercial infrastructure was to be redesigned to optimize profitability. The railway station was located in a privileged area, as soon more than 122,000 rail passengers would pass through this station every single day. Some would begin or end their journeys here, whereas others would change trains and have time to spare. And here, too, at the northernmost underpass, groups of people would scatter both above and below ground, would move back and forth, in and out, up and down the platforms and trains before letting themselves be transported in all possible directions. All of this traffic, of course, meant that the rents would rise. This

building, moreover, had been constructed using the strictest cost-control methods. The three elements had been stacked pragmatically one on top of the other like the crates that the crane in the freight terminal piled up alongside the railway tracks. The directors of the real estate venture wished to rent out the first of these volumes—the ground floor—to a bank, a shopping center, and a fast-food stand for the masses of commuters and students from the neighboring institute. The second main element with three equally spaced floors was to house offices, while the third "box" was intended for high-end legal firms. After all, the top floors had the best views of the surrounding area as well as a touch of urban flair. For fear of spiraling construction costs, the client had insisted on standardized construction methods. It also had plans to build a second version of the building to generate even more profit, this time along the fire protection wall at the station's northern end. The former milk loading dock now housing the rail workers' canteen would be torn down to make way for the huge new building in which the missing floor would also be doubled.

"Mrs. Diabolo, if you would please excuse me. I have matters to attend to. Thank you for your visit."

Laura was at a loss to understand what was going on. Why was the company simply disregarding the significant income that her rather generous offer would entail? Did those at the top realize—like Laura herself—that this building, as unspectacular as it was and with so many standardized elements looking as if it had come straight off the rack, was somehow trying to hide its immense volume? Wasn't it clear that it held a secret, and that the secret had something to do with the hidden floor? She could not have been the only person to have noticed that the facade seemed to react differently to external light and shade. It was as if the building were trying to communicate something about its interior via its exterior. Was this building really the first of its kind—a new type of architecture that could outwardly reflect not only its own creation and the history of the place, but also the mental state of its occupants? Could it be that she, Laura Diabolo, was the only one interested in the building's unusual capabilities? After all, the structure had an entirely different effect on its surroundings, even though its banal appearance meant that most people failed to even register its presence, despite its monumentality.

Gisèle stares at the strange red book in amazement. She turns it over and tries to make out a title on the front or back cover. Nothing. Could this be some sort of travel guide to Winterthur, she wonders? And isn't she herself now sitting in a shop located in the very same building? She has barely had the time to formulate the question in her mind before she finds herself getting up and hurrying outside to the other side of the street. She recognizes details such as the silver and anthracite-colored, shiny and matte shades of steel and aluminum, the strip of exterior cladding—described in the book as a transom band—

that covers the ground floor and spans the roof projecting out over the stairs. Contemplating the line of the building, she realizes that the projecting roof really is much higher than would be necessary if that was all it was. So the story in the book about the extra floor no longer seems so implausible after all. She wonders why a building might require such a farfetched story to get itself noticed and anchor itself in the public consciousness—if it was simply a way of getting people used to the unusual.

It begins to rain more heavily, and Gisèle hurries back to her table. Unable to continue where she left off since the pages are still soaked through, she starts to read at random towards the end of the book.

Without really noticing, the first janitor Hansueli Oklam rubbed harder than ever on the hemisphere hidden underneath the cladding fronting the mezzanine floor. Oklam was standing on a 20-foot-high safety scaffold that enabled him to comfortably reach the projecting roof. He had erected the scaffold at the regulation distance from pedestrian flows and had blocked it off with red and white barriers at precisely the same spot at which observant passersby always tended to stop when they wished to inspect the building more closely. They wondered what the fifteen protruding steel elements on the face of the projecting roof were for. No sooner had an art-savvy insurance officer floated the idea that it was some kind of artistic intervention than the wildest theories started circulating, ranging from trendy curtains and installations to movable facade elements that begin to waft as a result of the increase in air pressure brought about by trains entering the station.

In the course of his never-ending battle against pigeon droppings, however, Oklam had discovered by accident that one of the metal plates was equipped with an inside hinge that allowed it to be folded up. Behind the plate was a hemisphere made of crystal and as he began to polish the crystal, he suddenly felt himself being drawn into the story of the building's history. This month, too, he had taken his red polishing cloth from his pocket as he had done countless times before and as he began to rub the ball's surface he had found himself being sucked into the story of the missing mezzanine. This was the story that the crystal ball told him this time:

Despite all our scientifically tested measurements and calculations, when we attempted to lower the first block onto the property, it sank into the ground next to the railway tracks, tilted up, and remained irretrievably stuck. All of our attempts to salvage the block were of no avail. There followed numerous debates over what to do next. Then a taxi driver joined in the discussions. The invasion of bicycles that descended daily on the area—what, are we living in China now?—had made the station very difficult to access. There were simply too many cyclists standing around, too many looking for a place to lock up their bicycles, and too many racing round the bend at breakneck speed. Why

not use the opportunity to construct an underground bicycle garage?

The planning commission was enthusiastic, so we left a part of the slope that had been created as it was and converted it into an access ramp. We then laid concrete to smooth out all of the uneven spots and form a thick, load-bearing foundation. The result was a spacious, comfortable, and well-marked parking garage for 800 bicycles. There was even a staffed cleaning station on hand to give bicycles a quick wash. A large gateway granted direct access to the platforms via the pedestrian underpass under the tracks and it was this that earned the garage the name "From Saddle to Seat." In recognition of the idea that had saved the whole project, the client was generous to the taxi drivers: addressing their most basic human needs, it had a restroom installed exclusively for them, like the one for the police.

The first ground floor building was then placed atop the new foundation. This box, towering 15 feet above ground level, was covered with a roof that by projecting out to the south sheltered the stairs leading down to the pedestrian underpass. But when the roof was lowered into place, the transom band gave way, tore through the projecting roof and frayed outwards. The projecting roof thus expanded to become a mezzanine floor.

A sudden shrill cry brought Oklam back to the here and now: "Stubborn stuff, isn't it? They should make pigeons illegal." An elderly woman seemed to have been observing Oklam for some time as he worked away at the crystal ball.

Gisèle once again sets the red book down on the table. She has never read such an absurd story—about a building! What was the point of such a fantastic tale? And yet here she is, sitting most likely directly over the bicycle garage! Could the stacked arrangement of boxes that made up this building really have a story to tell? Was that the reason she found the strange book so captivating? Surprised at herself, she immediately opens the book at the next readable page and allows herself to be drawn into yet another story.

Oklam polished the crystal ball like a man possessed. He couldn't say whether he was dreaming or if he really did hear a voice speaking to him. It was as if the all of the stories and all of their many layers had been pressed together only to peel apart again and recombine in surprising new forms—visible in all their depth only on the surface of the crystal ball:

There were countless objects stored in this many-chambered underground storeroom. The objects were what remained of the town of Vitudurum's hard-fought battle for economic viability. For too long Vitudurum had found itself caught between the powerful free thinkers of Turicum on the one side and the staid Swiss Confederation on the other. This had been followed by an era of strict government control that had stymied all urban development. Yet with typical Swiss industriousness and hard work, Vitudurum in the late nineteenth century had managed to transform itself into an aspiring industrial town. Encouraged by this turn of events, the town fathers had set about building a railway to connect the town to the trade hubs to the east and west—and circumvent Turicum. But they had overplayed their hand, and the railway line was soon forced into liquidation. Whatever could be saved from seizure was hidden underground, especially if it contained raw materials or new technologies that would be of use in the future: wrought iron, fire engines, pumps, machines, parts of steam locomotives, and the very first diesel engines, rails, switches, and all sorts of heavy, large-scale iron tools all "disappeared," creating a cabinet of curiosities which has remained undiscovered to this day.

Oklam paused. He started to wonder about what he had just seen, and as soon as he stopped, the story in the crystal ball began to fade away into nothingness. "Could it really be true?" he thought to himself as he stood atop the scaffold. "Did they really lay the foundation of the new building on top of these catacombs? Surely the engineers who tested everything else would have noticed? Or maybe the stories told by the crystal ball were beyond the realm of what can be measured using science?"

Oklam glanced over at the station clock. He had now been cleaning the cladding for several hours, but he still had time for one more story from the crystal ball. So he went back to polishing it and the following story unfolded before his eyes:

The third and uppermost construction element was offset so that it projected out away from the station and over the sidewalk, giving the street a marker that delimited the northern boundary of the train station square.

"Wouldn't it be nice if Vitudurum finally did get its public square?" Oklam thought to himself. Suddenly his ringing cell phone tore him away from the story. After finishing a short telephone conversation, he climbed down from the scaffold and stood on the square, which in reality did not exist, but was actually just a fantasy in the minds of ambitious industrialists and urban planners.

Gisèle is dumbstruck. She pays for her coffee, packs away the fresh loaf of bread, her bundle of newspapers, and the red book into a bag and leaves the shop. She stares dry-eyed at the upper floors jutting out over the town and then walks as if in a trance to the corner of the building, where she inspects the anthracite-colored fire protection wall to the north, persuades herself of the reality of the ramp leading down into the bicycle garage, and steps out onto the westernmost platform. Although impressed by the fine-mesh safety barrier on the bicycle ramp and the newly designed train station, she is a bit taken aback by the out-of-place advertisements on the expressive raw concrete wall. Without realizing it, she walks around the entire building before returning to the place on the curb where she originally found the book. Still wondering whether or not she should keep the unsettling book now tucked away in her bag, she crosses the street, allowing herself to be guided by the idea that she is actually crossing a public square that in reality does not exist. But for Gisèle in that moment it is as real as it could ever be.

Schaffhausen

N1/N7

Basel

Zürich

P Süd   556
P Schützenwiese 147
P Bahnhof   148

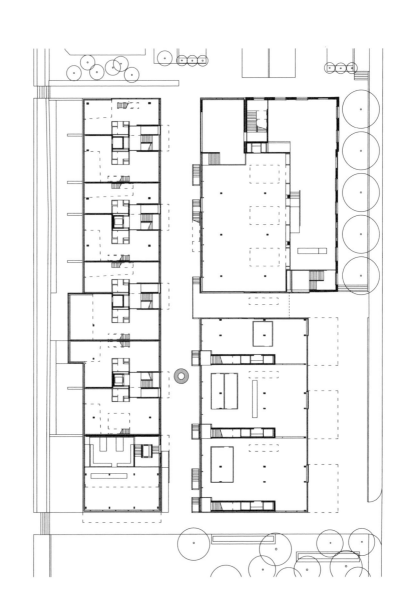

TREICHLER
MEETS SEMPER

BENJAMIN MUSCHG

Waschanstalt Wollishofen is an ambiguous building—or could it even be two or three buildings? One of the few things that can be said about it with any certainty is that it is no longer a laundry. And even that might be doubted by passersby on the lakeshore who, strolling past what could easily be mistaken for a converted 1960s office block, suddenly espy the familiar logo lurking behind its facade: a rooster clad in white with a stand-up collar and swagger stick standing stiffly in front of a yellow sky and strangely post-apocalyptic body of jet-black water reaching all the way up to his neck. But Waschanstalt Zürich AG moved out in 1997, abandoning the premises that company founder Heinrich Treichler had himself designed. Various parts of the complex have been demolished, enlarged, developed, converted, integrated, and rebuilt since then; yet the Waschanstalt has managed to survive.

The owner of the plot, the private bank Lienhardt & Partner, commissioned three architecture firms to produce studies, stipulating that they should include clear references to the laundry's history. In fact, the Zurich Office for Urban Development, which together with the bank originated the concept, viewed the laundry's history as worthier of preservation than the actual buildings. The architects were faced with the unconventional yet challenging task of reinventing the laundry, not merely by analytically preparing the terrain for their architectural design, but by making it an integral part of that design. A rusty piece of iron about the size of a hand that surfaced in 1999 during preliminary excavation work illustrates why the Waschanstalt is perfect for this design experiment, since it shows how the laundry was literally built on its own history.

The find turned out to be a relic of the sunken ship which housed the first Waschanstalt on the Limmatquai in downtown Zurich. It was there, in the 1850s, that Heinrich Treichler, a boatbuilder and owner of a charter company from Wädenswil, wanted to establish a floating laundry using state-of-the-art machinery. When the authorities were skeptical, Treichler approached no less a figure than the renowned architect Gottfried Semper. This kind of commission had never been seen

before, and was of little consequence for Semper, who was working at the time on a new main building for Zurich's Federal Polytechnic Institute. As the first architecture professor at what is now the Swiss Federal Institute of Technology, better known as the ETH Zurich, Semper was nevertheless curious enough to set his students the task of producing a design, and ultimately came up with a laundry boat of his own. In 1864, the finished vessel docked at what is now Hechtplatz, and despite being little more than a raft still counts as a classic example of Semper's concept of polychrome architecture and theory of cladding.

The floating washing machine was approximately 72 feet long, 30 feet wide, and 13 feet high. It had a slightly tapered hull, a deck with a railing running all round the vessel, and a somewhat barrel-shaped roof, all of which gave it a boat-like appearance. The supporting iron

structure was infilled with wood on the inside and sheet metal on the
outside; the facade was painted with colorful Pompeian motifs, and
there were artfully molded cast-iron elements, such as the forty-two
kore-like figures supporting the roof. The design of the external shell
and symbolism of the motifs made Semper's work closer to architecture than boatbuilding. By extending the idea of architecture to a construction that was neither permanent nor stationary, this leading nine-
teenth-century architect showed himself to be a true visionary. Sixty
years later, Le Corbusier chided his fellow architects for ignoring the in-
finitely larger transatlantic steamers.

   Only eight years after Semper's colorful vessel moored at the Limmatquai, it was forced to move to make way for the new quayside built
in 1872. Treichler had the boat towed to the waterfront of the then independent suburb of Wollishofen, where he already owned a house and
dockyard. When he was granted permission two years later to occupy
the entire area of what now comprises the laundry premises, the hull
of the laundry boat promptly became part of the embankment, and its
colorful superstructure the first floor of the laundry. In the years that
followed, the rapidly expanding company laid claim to more and more
of the land on either side of Semper's vessel. Around the turn of the
century, another strip of land was added to the rear along
the whole length of the lakeside buildings, while the two-
story extension with its brick facade along the street was
added in 1906. By that time, the boat had been swallowed
up by its surroundings, with only its convex tin roof
glimpsed between the gabled shed roofs and a single facade
facing the lake still visible. The other facades had become
intrusive internal partitions and were removed altogether
in the 1920s to create a larger continuous working space.

   The floating laundry survived for nearly a century as
part of the patchwork-style development and redevelop-

Arbeitsräume bezüglich Helligkeit und Luftigkeit. Die Arbeits-
atmosphäre würde nicht allein im renovierten Teil, sondern im
ganzen Parterre günstig beeinflusst. Alles wäre wesentlich lichter
und freundlicher.
Wichtig ist der Gewinn an Arbeitsfläche zwecks Lockerung und
Verbesserung der Arbeitsplätze im Parterre.

Nach aussen erhielte man Gebäulichkeiten, die sich sehen lassen
dürften.

Seeansicht heute.

neue Seeansicht.

Bitte zu beachten :

Die Wirkung der Bauhöhe bleibt gleich ! Von der Seeseite ge-
sehen wird die Höhe unserer Gebäulichkeiten schon heute durch
die 2-stöckigen Bauten an der Seestrasse bestimmt !

ment that soon spread over the entire lakeside plot. It was not until 1960 that the remains were scrapped during the last major company expansion when the single-story buildings along the lakefront were replaced by a two-story steel-frame construction. Laundry was still washed on the site for almost another four decades before the company fell victim to market forces. Once the industrial laundry was no longer profitable, it was replaced by a mixture of offices, small businesses, exclusive residences, and restaurants. When renovation work began in 1999, this piece of riveted wreckage was raised from the bottom of the lake and now counts as the sole remaining relic of Semper's laundry boat. Discovered just in time for the bicentenary of his birth, the section of the hull even went on tour, and in 2003 was exhibited in Zurich and Munich (cat. no. 88) as evidence of an odd, yet programmatic work by the renowned architect.

The story of Semper's boat is probably the most bizarre of all the many episodes engraved on the palimpsest of the Waschanstalt Wollishofen. Remodeling the site actually involved coming up with a blueprint for a rereading of its history. It is a venture that architecture can risk only because it "is privileged to have something to do with almost everything and an understanding of almost nothing," as Marcel Meili commented in an essay on the conversion of an old factory into a residential and commercial building in Zurich. Every design, Meili continued, is a mercurial speculation on the history of architecture; which is why he approaches a commission by attempting "to free myself from any prejudice or supposed prior knowledge to the extent that we can sense the subtle, hidden, and unknown appeal of the task in hand." If the architect succeeds in approaching a commission as a true amateur, with the necessary degree of naivety, then "reading" the building's story can become a creative process, the first draft of an architectural attitude. Meili's text on the conversion was published only in 2001, although the project itself was completed in 1997. Perhaps it is no coincidence that it reads like a strategy for converting the Waschanstalt written after the fact. The offices of agps are located in the very same building that Meili describes.

The collage-style method adopted for planning the conversion of the Waschanstalt followed a particular reading of its evolutionary history; in other words, it was reinterpreted with appropriate additive and reductive techniques. The site had originally been constructed and developed according to the economic, technical, and commercial needs of the industrial laundry, but its more recent incarnation demanded that very different criteria be followed. In line with earlier structural changes, the existing elements and buildings were assessed purely in terms of their future utility rather than their specific features, and were then removed, altered, or retained as appropriate. There was no requirement that the changes made should either blend in with the remaining structures or stand out from them. This approach led to a heterogeneous project that was both conversion and construction, on the one hand alluding to the history of the laundry, while on the other hand breaking with the past, and by doing so becoming a new whole. For whereas the preexisting collage developed autonomously over a substantial period of time, the one-off, intentional intervention "froze" it as a fixed composition.

The site was already divided into zones running parallel to the lakeshore and street, and this organization was retained for the new mixed-use development. The strip of land facing the street became a two-story office and commercial space, linking the Waschanstalt site to the public space of the open-air swimming pool adjoining it to the north. It also served as a noise barrier for the row of housing along the lakefront which, at almost double the height, extends the line of villas to the south. The housing volume along the lakeside is 72 feet wide and hence commensurate with Semper's long-gone laundry boat. The office and residential buildings are entered from the new alleyway between them, which is situated where the two sections of the old laundry were connected.

Whereas the method and structure of the design contain much of the Waschanstalt's history, no more than a tenth of the preexisting structure was retained, and even less than that is visible. The systematic play of ambiguity and internal contradictions that once operated in the Waschanstalt is self-evidently demonstrated by this historical point of reference. Only three structural elements were retained and reused when the site was redeveloped: the brick facade in the southwest corner, the chimney stack, and the steel frame of the lakeside building. The 1929 filter tower, however, was demolished, even if this concrete monolith still appears to be protruding out of the curtain wall facing the lake. The erstwhile filter tower exists  only as an omission in the surviving steel structure; the replica of the tower, although in the same position as the original and forming an integral part of the facade assembly, does not follow the internal structure of the duplex and loft apartments behind it, nor even that of their rooms.

According to a publication to mark the company's centenary, André E. Bosshard's modernist design of 1960 fulfilled the Waschanstalt's "long cherished wish" to replace the "old, ramshackle, one-story premises along the lakefront" with a "much larger and more attractive" building. In the course of its conversion, the building was stripped down to its steel frame, the very same feature that had facilitated the large open-plan areas and spared the company from having to use the smaller buildings on either side of Semper's boat. Although the dimensions of the center lines on the new facade are based on Bosshard's load-bearing structure, it was overlaid with a system of continuous shear walls connected by concrete slabs. The concrete supporting walls that cantilever a meter beyond the steel frame to the rear divide the apartments, reconstructing the former structure of parallel spaces at right angles to the lake within the same frame. The shear panels are placed at alternating intervals to the steel frame so that the frame itself is visible even inside the apartments.

Anyone who saw the brick building facing the street complete with the Waschanstalt lettering and logo would believe it to be an authentic relic of the bygone industrial epoch, and might even feel hoodwinked on finding it to house a modern reinforced concrete structure inside the brickwork. Yet the deception is an original feature—the bricks were after all added as cladding for the run-of-the-mill concrete structure erected in 1906.

The 100-foot-high chimney stack shooting straight out of the ground these days emits far more industrial charm than smoke. An unmistakable symbol, it seems to flaunt the purposelessness of its existence and the fact that it has become a meeting point for young urban professionals. Although no longer needed for its original function, it has acquired three new ones since the conversion: first it divides the alleyway between the parallel blocks into a public area with restaurants, offices, and studios to the north, and a private area to the south, where the entrances to the apartments are located; second, the fumes from the restaurant and kitchen exhaust system are dispersed through the chimney; and third, its crown has been redesigned as a nesting site for swifts, a bird whose lifestyle resembles that of the young, urban professional: both spend a large part of their lives up in the air, and when they do come down to earth, show a marked preference for urban industrial wastelands.

Continuing this exploration of the connection between old and new structures as well as collage techniques seemed an obvious step for the architects in later projects. Two years after the Waschanstalt conversion was completed, work began on the conversion of the Kormann-

Stüber residence perched above the "Gold Coast" in Küsnacht on the opposite side of Lake Zurich. The ambiguities of the Waschanstalt stemmed from the change of function and drastic modifications made to the fabric of the buildings, whereas this family home was to retain both its original function and to a large extent its shape. If the Waschanstalt can be described as a "temporally open composition," to use Meili's expression, the transformation of the Küsnacht villa, which was constructed as a prestigious country house, can be labeled a conscious falsification of perception.

By stripping the Kormann-Stüber house bare and then applying a new layer to a virtually unchanged structure, the architects were able to create the illusion of a contemporary new building. The first step was to take the outer siding off the 1930s reinforced concrete structure and to remove the gables from the flat concrete roof to reveal the raw structure. The second step was to reorganize the building by lowering the garage and installing a central HVAC system; by extending the upper floor on top of the L-shaped lower floor with a ten-foot-wide "rucksack"; and by replacing the porthole windows with horizontal clerestory glazing. Finally, although the

total amount of space had hardly changed, the house was given a radical facelift with facades of different colors and materials. The architects were not even above resorting to cheap tricks to achieve the desired effect, among them the mirror on the facade which makes the roof edge of the lower part of the building appear to run right though behind the two-story section.

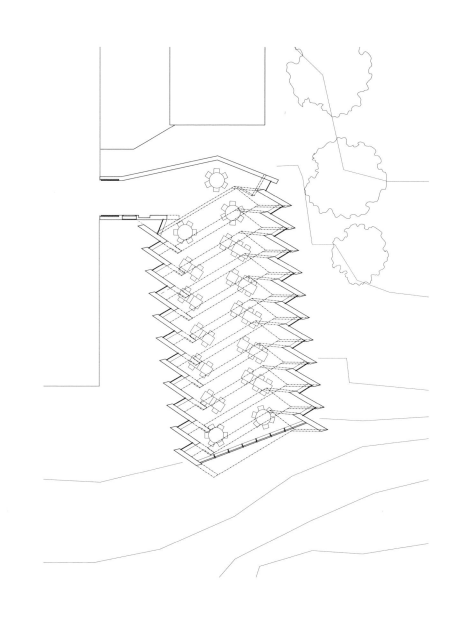

BUTTERFLY IN MOUNTAIN SCENERY

VERENA DOERFLER

Blame it all on art. Or rather on a gallery owner. Or rather on the wife—who happens to be a gallery owner—of one of the members of the hotel's managing board. She was the one who insisted on the change.

Hotel Hof Weissbad is located in the picturesque Swiss canton of Appenzell at the foot of the Alpstein Mountains. With its grass-green meadows, rippling streams, jagged mountains, and twittering birds, it is a place in the middle of nowhere. But a setting as if made for a health resort. Thanks to the canniness of the locals, the hotel has been almost completely booked out for the last several years and is thus a "self-supporting" business, as those in the hotel industry would say. To guarantee a steady stream of guests, the owners gave the hotel its own spa, and to get health insurers on board, a "hotel clinic" complete with medical staff. Guests can thus simultaneously relax and recover in the glamorous atmosphere of this seemingly classical hotel. Rising numbers of guests, however, meant that the hotel's dining facilities became rather cramped over the course of time. Realizing that the rustic dining room, the "Schotte-Sepp-Stobe," was virtually bursting at the seams at peak season, the managing board decided on an expansion.

It was at this point that our gallery owner raised an objection: Might it not be time for something new? And suddenly the million-dollar question was on the table. Luckily she knew an architect, or rather, she was the former gallerist of an artist whose husband just happened to be a noteworthy Zurich-based architect… It is always individuals, and frequently individuals at odds with the conventions of the day, who are the instigators of new and unusual architecture.

It is at any rate the artist Blanca Blarer who for many years has contributed to the rather different symbiosis of art and architecture that characterizes many of the architectural designs by agps. And as a patroness of art ensconced in a remote and mountainous region, Agathe Nisple, Blarer's former gallerist, epitomizes what could be called an Appenzeller contradiction. Those who visit her home are soon aware that it has very little to do with traditional Appenzell-style abodes. First of all, there is not a hint of folklore, nor is there any sense of mountain seclusion. The house receives a great number of visitors: not only artists and curators from far away, but also the neighbors from next-door. On Saturdays Agathe regularly hosts a kind of "open house," for which she needs no real occasion other than her need to indulge in a bit of conviviality. Visitors meet for a chat and to enjoy their weekends off. For Mrs. Nisple, art is truly something of a way of life. So the house and hostess are anything other than typically Appenzell.

Nor is Hotel Hof Weissbad "typically Appenzell," at least not in terms of architecture. Seemingly rather plain and solid, it is a yellow-painted sprawling expanse of a building surrounded by a field of permanent green, speckled with touches of white. The first-time visitor is not quite sure of what to expect—a glamorous and opulent spa hotel or just a simple mountain retreat. Seen from outside, the architecture refuses to let on one bit.

Approaching the entrance, the guest is greeted with the words "Appenzell & Gesundheit" (Appenzell & Health), which is at least indicative of what awaits inside. The interior welcomes with a rush of cream-colored curtains, heavily upholstered furniture, a few hand-carved decorations—and an exceedingly friendly staff. Christian Lienhard is the hotel's resourceful director. And yes, Mr. Lienhard also had a role in letting in the fresh architectural breeze that is currently blowing about the area's peaks.

Mr. Lienhard is the progressive type of hotelier—one who knows that no hotel can remain attractive forever. The magic word is "modernization," creating incentives, always being a step ahead of the rest. This, at any rate, is his short and simple recipe for success. Cultural and artistic interventions aimed at offering a temporary respite from the regular program are just one of the numerous starting points in this endeavor. A good example of this is provided by the art of native Appenzeller Roman Signer: a barrel stands in the hotel's first-floor foyer into which rainwater is channeled through a funnel on the roof. Too bad for the guest—a woman of pedigree perhaps—who mistakes the barrel filled to the brim with water for a perfect place to set down her designer handbag. Bye bye Dior!

The fact that Mr. Lienhard can smile at such misappropriations of art is proof both of his humor as well as a certain openness—openness toward the unpredictable. Which is not at all a bad trait to have, and was again in evidence when Mr. Lienhard was presented with the plans for the hotel's new dining room by a Zurich-based firm of architects. There was talk of wooden arches and strip glazing, of prefabricated construction materials and a completely new sense of space. At first it was all a bit difficult for the layman to understand—hence the importance of Mr. Lienhard's fondness for experimentation.

The dining room's architecture was inspired by the Goldzack rubber-band factory in nearby Gossau. The unusual design and construction of this well-lit factory hall built in 1955 were the work of the architect Heinrich Danzeisen and engineer Heinz Hossdorf. The design was simple in principle, but impressive in terms of space. Inclined arch elements were erected in a rhythmic progression that made it appear as if the entire construction were about to tumble over, with only glass to hold them together. When seen from the side, the building looks completely open, yet when viewed from the ends, the exact opposite is true. So far so good, even if explaining it to the layman is not so easy. The people of Weissbad proved their courage and willingness to abandon tradition for the sake of renewal when they approved the construction plans for the new extension. And this despite Mrs. Nisple's legitimate insistence and Mr. Lienhard's well-documented openness.

Construction was completed in just six short weeks. First a concrete foundation was laid deep in the earth to the left of the hotel, and then the prefabricated arches began arriving. Glass was inserted both to connect the arches and to ensure plenty of incident light. The last step was the addition of the scale-like zinc cladding.

For the locals, the fact that a woman had played a leading role in the creation of this "unbelievable" work of architecture erected during the summer holidays was nearly as sensational as the building itself. But perhaps the challenge in its entirety also offered something of an incentive for the people of this region—a kick start for the notion of "doing things differently in Appenzell"?

"Different" is definitely the right word to describe the hotel's new extension. Looking from a distance like a giant steel reptile in a green and mountainous landscape, the restaurant named Flickflauder— meaning butterfly in local dialect—represents something both singular and strange is this alpine region. But then again, "normal" would have most likely been the wrong place to start, and the same could be said of the Flickflauder's interior.

In yet another example of openness, what at first looks like a wall turns out to be an expanse of windows with polished panes of glass anchored at the floor. It is the perspective that counts! How else could we explain the story told to us by a server about how a guest had recently walked head-on into one of the windows. A certain degree of easy-going humor in light of such confusion (not only artistic, but architectural, too,) is clearly a must—particularly on the part of the guest, we hope. After all, navigating new architectural and artistic spaces requires a degree of modesty, and that, too, is something that can be learned.

The Flickflauder's unusual interior is more than just a cause for confusion, however. There is something almost sacred about the space,

something—one hardly dares to write it—transcendental, which most likely is a result of the incident light and the panes of glass that connect the eleven arches. The senses certainly find it confusing when subjected to what seems like sunlight coming in from all sides at once, especially as it is not so easy to make out where the wall ends and the ceiling begins. The view from the inside out is not only pleasing, but there is something uplifting about it, too. It is no accident that the architects arranged the space so that every guest at one of the crooked rows of tables would have an unimpeded view of the famed Hoher Kasten and its surrounding peaks.

All in all, the new dining room is a hit even with the guests who flock to the hotel in search of relaxation. The "Schotte-Sepp-Stobe" in the main building now seems almost desolate compared with the modern elegance of the Flickflauder. The new dining room lends the classical spa hotel a note of extravagance and contemporary distinction. The first-class cuisine takes care of the rest.

Whether the locals will take to this wholly newfangled yet profit-able addition to their village set against a perpetually green alpine back-drop remains to be seen. That Flickflauder—the architectural butter-fly—has been accepted by the tradition-conscious older residents as a welcome departure from the norm does at least speak for human flex-ibility, if not much more.

The locals are full of pride for this new architectural feat, and are happy with the village's collective courage in bringing about a new phase of edificial renewal. Perhaps it is precisely because art follows its own particular rhythm in these mountains that people here are com-pletely open to the idea of change. Even if many a deluded child of the city sometimes sees things differently.

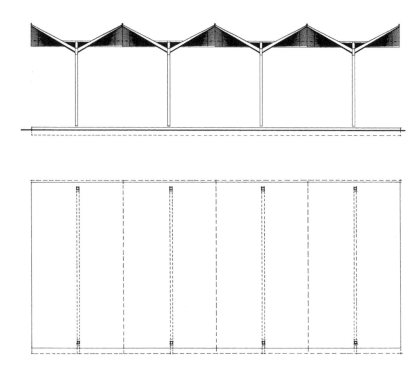

CREATURES ON THE TIPS OF THEIR TOES

DENISE BRATTON

Arriving in Los Angeles in the late 1980s, the architects cast a wide net in their search for work. One objective was to secure a project with the Los Angeles Unified School District (LAUSD), the second largest metropolitan school district in the country after New York City. Getting an interview with the LAUSD in 1989 turned out to be relatively easy, and in short order the architects had a commission to design pavilions to shelter lunch areas for children on the grounds of fifty public school throughout the city. From the outset, the need to accommodate very different site conditions was built into the program; at the same time, budget constraints and the mandate for a minimum installation time suggested that the "lunch shelters," as the architects came to call them, be conceived on a template that could be prefabricated, mass produced, and easily assembled on site. The very temperate climate of Los Angeles dictated that shade, rather than shelter from rain, would be the primary function these structures had to fulfill.

At the time, LAUSD was responsible for close to 600,000 schoolchildren speaking fifty-seven different languages, and thus was obliged to standardize its programs to ensure that basic services were available to all. In addition to growing public awareness that not only the physical fabric of the district's public schools, but also the quality and character of education itself was in decline, the lunch shelters project may also have coincided with a dawning consciousness of the importance of nutrition in the lives of schoolchildren and the corollary social problem that few children actually share even one meal a day with their families. To put things into perspective, one grammar school principal laid out her personal objectives as hygiene, nutrition, and education—in that order.

The "facts" of the project were an assortment of rather bleak and desolate school grounds and a dire lack of funding for infrastructural amenities. Just a quarter of a century after the Watts Riots and just prior to the civil unrest that exploded across Los Angeles in 1992, social inequities were rife in a megacity where economic disparity was, and still is, most evident in public schools. In some communities, schools can be described as plain; in others, they are not only bleak but also dangerous. In Watts, for example, schools simmer with neglected and discontented youth. Any structures installed on school grounds suffer a beating of one form or another from everyday use to tagging by graffiti. The shelters would have to stand up to all this and more. And given the high degree of mobility that characterizes LA's population at large, there was an expectation that the lunch shelters would have to migrate around the city on an as-needed basis.

The architects studied the striking variety of site conditions across the city, looking at topography, ground surface, scale, and landscape for the schools they visited. They closely observed how "lunch period" transpires, how children behave when they are eating, and what happens during the rest of the day on the sites designated for the new structures. While measuring one site, Sarah Graham was shocked to witness, not surprisingly in Watts, what might have been a drive-by shooting: an explosive noise that caused all the children on the playground to hit the ground for protection; she alone was left standing, incredulous as she watched the children pick themselves up and resume playing their games, apparently unfazed. The architects brought to this project an ethos inclined to social justice, a belief that architecture can be a force for good, no matter how minor the intervention; and in the case of the lunch shelters, they also sought to infuse the project with a sense of *play* to enliven the daily routine of the children and perhaps even to inspire them.

From research and observation, and a design process that became an exercise in difference and repetition, the team produced a whole battery of possible schemes and models addressing the generic brief calling for a roof mounted on a concrete slab outfitted with a drain as well as tables and benches that could be bolted down. These were unveiled at a meeting with district administrators, all of whom were managers rarely exposed to thorough design investigation. It caused something of a stir and gathered a crowd of onlookers. In some ways, this was evidence of how impoverished public school architecture had become over decades and decades of economic cutbacks and public disinterest, despite a number of fine examples built in the United States after the Second World War. In response to the proposed schemes, the clients began to refine the brief as administrators added various constraints: beware of wild birds who like to build nests in open structures, and don't bother to incorporate landscaping because the predominant surface material for school grounds is asphalt, a material that is cheap, clean, and relatively safe when wet.

In their first experience collaborating with Ove Arup, Los Angeles, the architects devised a module for a roof constructed of doubly curved, light-gauge steel framed with straight, galvanized members;

the modules were designed to be clipped together laterally or longitudinally, depending on the site condition. A minimum of two modules joined together would attain stability; in multiples of two or more, they were designed to be pin-connected to the ground, hovering like folded paper dragons on long legs that touch the ground very lightly. The individual schools were invited to choose which color roof surface they preferred. With all of their structural elements and constructive means fully exposed from beneath, these almost surreal creatures become a "lesson" in themselves: children sitting at the lunch tables can easily apprehend their simple tectonic logic while munching on a sandwich.

Though the architects considered exploiting the potential of computer-integrated manufacturing to produce the modules, only subsequent projects in Europe allowed them to deploy such technologies. For the lunch shelters, the engineers developed a computer program to calculate and size the elements, each of which was unique. The program

could easily have been used for digitally controlled production, but as no local fabricator could be found to accomplish this task, the architects had no choice but to revert to traditional methods of construction.

The question of fabrication in two grades of steel sent the architects off in search of contractors who had the capacity to bridge two trades, working in both structural and light-gauge steel. The bidding process proved difficult, and introduced the architects to one of their persistent nightmares as designers working in the United States: substandard building practices devoid of any sense of craft—an industry in which the only art is the art of the low bid, the skill of cutting corners, and a devil-may-care attitude to quality. In stark contrast to most companies who submitted bids for the project, only one manufacturer seemed honest and able to comply with the meager budget available. Using an almost artisanal approach based on conventional cutting and welding techniques, he brought craftsmanship and dedication to the project. The construction was rough, but the result exceptionally powerful.

In the end, that cold call to LAUSD confirmed the architects' understanding of architectural space as a generator of social space. Once a few of the lunch shelters had been completed, the district began to comprehend this potential, and began making use of them for a wider range of purposes, including community functions as well as many different types of school-related meetings. For the children, the very presence of the lunch shelters was cause for anticipation that something interesting—not just something frightening—might occur on the school ground.

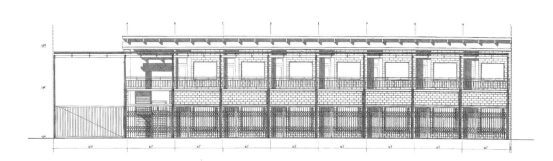

ALMOST INFORMAL

DENISE BRATTON

Architecture's potential to improve and unify its surrounding context is routinely exploited. Generally speaking, "moving architecture to the background" and "inviting users to take a role in defining a building" is more difficult; yet this is what agps decided to do with its Koreatown Storefronts project. In this instance, the architects had a dual agenda. On the one hand, the modest commission gave them an opportunity to design an "out-of-the-box" type of retail architecture on a scale and in a restrained design mode that would be appropriate in the context of a particularly generic neighborhood. This was as much a form of resistance to the bland, big-box stores that dominate the urban fabric and its surrounding suburbs as an attempt to find a role for architecture in a context where virtually none existed. On the other hand, the simple and flexible infrastructure the architects devised to "screen" the building facade was calculated to enhance the urban as well as the social sphere. Ironically, the completion of the Koreatown Storefronts in 1992 coincided with one of the most disturbing instances of urban unrest in the city's history.

The story began when the architects were approached by a handy-man who worked for the owner of the storefront on Melrose Avenue where they had set up offices. Mr. Fixel, a minor real estate developer, had sent his handyman over to fix a problem with the hot water heater. Motivated by an excess of curiosity, the handyman gathered what was going on in the studio, and suggested that the architects might contact his employer about a small commercial project he was developing in the neighborhood. Without further ado, they followed up the lead and were hired almost on the spot to design a commercial building with multiple storefronts.

Fixel himself had no particular knowledge of—or experience with—architecture, but this did not prevent him wanting to build. For the architects, the contradiction invoked something Frank Gehry once said: "I live and work in Los Angeles where it is possible to live one's entire life without seeing a work of architecture." In fact, the Koreatown community where Fixel's parcel was located was a working-class neigh-borhood inhabited mainly by immigrant Korean and Hispanic resi-dents, in which nondescript houses and apartment buildings were densely interspersed with all manner of small shops, many occupied by family-owned businesses. Most of these buildings were no doubt drawn up and built by contractors. As it turned out, the handyman—"a master of improvisation"—was also Fixel's contractor; the budget was low.

The architects designed a low-rise, two-story, wood-frame and masonry building that was ordinary in every respect except for its fa-cade. Here, exposed concrete block formed a series of bays punctuated with deeply hung windows that alternate with the recessed doorways marking the individual storefronts opening onto the street. Onto this strikingly simple, but in spite of itself elegant facade, the architects "clipped" a welded-steel frame assembly—a mask of sorts. The screen-like armature was to support signage and security hardware, banners, lighting, and even flags, which can be attached, detached, or rearranged as needs wax and wane according to changing circumstances. This was the first step in an ongoing process of adding layers to a building that will continue to change and evolve over time as it takes on the identity of its tenants and is adapted to the functions it must serve. The intent was for the building to become the "ground" for a palimpsest of lettering and messages that would ultimately be carried by the armature affixed to its facade.

Here again, as with many other projects, the construction phase became the crucible, with the handyman-contractor paying precision construction drawings only cursory attention. His tendency to rely on informal practices rather than applying himself to understanding the architects' intentions caused troublesome mishaps. The deep level at which the architects found this unsettling is directly attributable to their *formal* training—their commitment not only to the aesthetic, but

also to the craft and material qualities of architecture. In reality, however, a plethora of vernacular buildings of very *informal* origin makes up the cityscape of Los Angeles; rare is the building that can be regarded as well-designed and also well-made, and much of what one sees on street after street is the first layer of building ever to have been erected there. The project to design storefronts for a neighborhood where there was no expectation of beauty or craftsmanship moved the architects to pursue a "zero degree" in architecture akin to what Roland Barthes had argued for in literature as a practice, an *écriture*, that wants to be unobtrusive and to engage the reader or "user," inviting a kind of participation that remakes or redefines the work.

A cursory look around Koreatown, taking in the many ways in which ordinary stucco buildings are adapted ad hoc, modified, and even completely transformed by proprietors and passersby over time, reveals an informal process to which commercial and vernacular architecture submits itself rather willingly. With this project, the designers hoped to relegate architecture with a capital A to a minor role, setting the stage, so to speak, for the incalculable actions and reactions of users over what will undoubtedly be a long period of time. This stage-setting betrays an appreciation on their part of the quotidian, the ordinary, the discordant, even the ugly aspects of cities.

As fate would have it, the architects' projects in Los Angeles have each, in one way or another, functioned as lightning rods, illuminating architecture's relation or response to urban chaos. Once the Koreatown building had been completed, and while the client was still in the process of negotiating leases with prospective tenants, an outbreak of violent protest was ignited by a court decision in the matter of Rodney King on April 29, 1992. Of all the Los Angeles neighborhoods affected, Koreatown was particularly hard hit due to hostilities that had already reached the level of gang warfare between Koreans and African Americans. Only when the curfews were lifted and the dust began to settle after six days of violence and arson that had paralyzed many parts of the city did the architects venture out to have a look. What they found, amid the near-total destruction of all the other generic storefronts in the area, was that Fixel's brand new building had been left untouched. Its lack of visual association with anyone or anything, the very *absence* of identity, had spared it the torch amid conflagrations fueled by identity politics.

In the intervening years, as Fixel's building was painstakingly encoded with the signs of use and ethnicity, the storefronts were subsumed into the banal fabric of the city, their scaffolding so laden with competing identities that the building is now indistinguishable from the rest—but in this case by design.

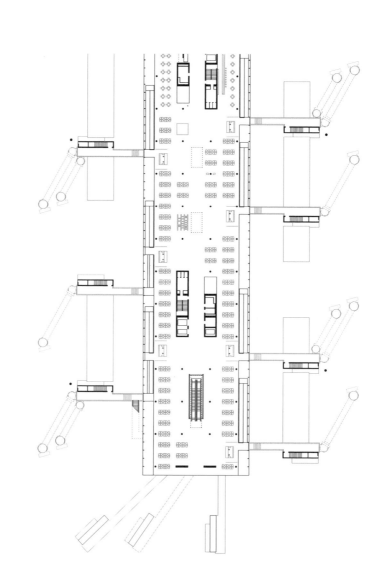

A PIANO IN THE ZEPPELIN

Benjamin Muschg

Every Wednesday afternoon, several individuals and small groups—almost exclusively older men—gather with their binoculars, cameras, and notepads and make the journey to Zurich International Airport which, although anything but unique, was once renamed Unique Airport. First they pay two Swiss francs to pass through security to the visitors' viewing area of Dock B (now called the Event Dock), and then, at the counter of the self-service restaurant, they buy a second ticket costing four francs which allows them to travel by shuttle bus through a tunnel over half a mile long to the middle of the runway triangle. There, a friendly employee escorts them into the elevator up to the roof of Dock Midfield, which now goes by the name of Dock E. The freedom up there is by no means unlimited—the planespotters are in the thick of things, yet utterly uninvolved. But for Swiss aviation fans, this 6,700-square-foot viewing deck at the southern end of a building about a third of a mile long is the ideal place to satisfy a desire wholly unknown to almost everyone else at the airport. Airports, of course, are not built just so that people can stand on a viewing deck spotting airplanes for hours on end, scribbling down their take-off and landing times, their airport of origin, and tail markings. In the competitive market of international airports, more and more of which are now doubling as shopping malls and leisure facilities, the observation deck is of negligible importance. But the

 qualities picked up by these possibly somewhat marginalized planespotters can be crucial to airport architecture: what others see as a fully automated means of transport is for them a dream of humanity come true; what others condemn as emissions and noise pollution, they relish as the smells and sounds of the wider world; where others see uniformity and desolation, they see diversity and wonder. Aviation fans focus not on the airport's necessities and economics, but on its very essence.

The men with the binoculars have an esoteric, naïve view of air traffic that is not necessarily shared by the airport's other users, whether employees, travelers, or shoppers. Indirect evidence of this can be found in the different reactions to *Airports*, a series of photographs by Peter Fischli and David Weiss. Most viewers will either shrug their shoulders or be puzzled by their large-format, high-definition images of the world's airports, for the motifs are banal, interchangeable, and lacking any aesthetic appeal, without either artistic aspirations or beauty. For someone used to decoding images of airports, playing with perception in this way is futile. Perhaps Fischli and Weiss's photos illustrate the grim reality of globalization—or show a sublime beauty that can be unlocked only by a few eccentrics equipped with binoculars, cameras, and notepads. As the saying goes, beauty lies in the eye of the beholder.

Architecture, however, can hardly be blamed for the fact that most people now regard the airport as a bleak non-place—an image alluded to by Fischli and Weiss in their images. Air travel itself was instrumental in debunking its own myth—at least once the advent of the jet

engine in the 1950s set in motion its seemingly unstoppable
growth. As flying was transformed from an adventure into
a global mass phenomenon, architecture fell by the wayside
and was left to languish along with both the passengers and
the environment. Whereas the economic boom in air traffic forced architecture to take a back seat during the second
half of the twentieth century, the nosedive the industry
went into around the millennium led to its resurgence. As
international competition grows ever tougher, architectural design is credited with a value-added which the expressive form of more recent buildings was intended to increase; a unique appearance can be a powerful marketing
tool, making a building stand out from the crowd and giving it that "instant recognition" factor.

Yet a newspaper article published in 2003 just after
Dock E opened, accused it of failing to achieve precisely
that. Felix Müller complained about the lack of prestigious
buildings in Zurich, citing the new airport terminal as an
example of "architecture by the book," characterized by "a high utility
value, elegant aesthetics, discreet modernism, and rational design."
While the building cannot conclusively be described in this manner,
these characteristics do represent an idealized form of Zurich's puri-
tanical, Zwinglian spirit which according to the article stifles prestigious
architecture. Paradoxically, it is the absence of a "special form" that
gives Dock E the authenticity and uniqueness that the operator of
Zurich airport proclaims on its flags.

A conscious decision was made to find a formal manifestation
for Dock E that reflected everyday appearances rather than expressive
formal qualities. Entering the building, you can see this "poetry of
the everyday" (to use the architects' expression) in the raw materials
used; in the well-planned sequencing of the areas passengers must pass

through on their way to and from the plane; in the handling of daylight; and in the grand vistas of the airfield and the surroundings. Visitors are confronted with other, similarly unadorned expressions of daily life, too: an abundance of advertising, shopping, fast food, and the stressed-out people who are the target of hard-sell consumerism.

Perhaps the concept of the "poetry of the everyday" is nowhere near as important for the finished building as it was for defining the project's goals. The expression sounds appealing and is vague enough to absorb a range of interests and changing specifications for the project as organism. Unlike a formal vision, this vague definition encourages discussion, and provides a forum for the ideas of all involved parties. Consequently, the core idea may stand for a conceptual and communicative culture that not only indicates which direction should be taken, but also stimulates new ideas. Surprising associations from one area can bear fruit in another or become leitmotifs for the entire project.

A good example of this is the story of the piano in the Zeppelin, which came up during an early exchange of ideas. The engineer who told the tale found it fascinating that the *Hindenburg*, an LZ 129 Zeppelin that was a technical miracle in its times and at 800 feet long and 150 feet in diameter the largest airship ever built, still carried a grand piano for entertaining its passengers. The luxury of a grand piano was affordable only because it was specially built of aluminum, like the airship itself. The putative moral of the story is that even an object as heavy as a grand piano can be taken on board an airship if the designer can disassociate the object from all preconceptions pertaining to it—and simply build a lighter piano. But the truth is that a piano would never have been considered at all if the engineers' ideas had been followed to the letter. The Zeppelin was built to contain helium instead of hydrogen, as previous models had done. The political situation in 1936 was so tense, however, that the helium required could not be imported from the USA, with the result that highly flammable hydrogen was used after all. And it was hydrogen's higher load-bearing capacity that allowed more weight to be transported on the airship.

Both lessons from the tale of the piano on the Zeppelin have been applied to the design of Dock E. The first shows how innovative solutions can be found by looking at familiar things from a new perspective, which in turn can lead to economically and architecturally purposeful multiple utilizations. To take two examples: the 440 foundation piles that had to be driven 100 feet into the earth were not just structural, but a means of generating energy as well, while the service areas at the front with ramps leading down from the departure level to the airplanes double as climatic buffers.

The other lesson is that sometimes even mishaps and misunderstandings yield good solutions. The roof pergola, for example was originally intended to provide shade for the exposed south facade. But when it took on a life of its own as an all-round roof at the planning stage, the

architects realized it would permit a significantly larger photovoltaic system, while at the same time improving the overall architectural impact of the building. In the words of American author Joseph Heller: "Nothing succeeds as planned," but the result is often much better when reality intervenes.

The piano in the Zeppelin also stands for the surreal and the unreal. There are surprises in store in every nook and cranny of Dock E: small courtyards with no particular function bearing vines and creepers from every continent; shimmering shards of blue glass used instead of gravel; skillfully worked wooden handrails on parapets and balustrades; artificial blue light on blue ramps; a coat of silver paint in the stairwells; walls painted red to highlight the signage system; iridescent views through freestanding partition walls. At first glance these elements are merely nondescript; at second glance slightly perplexing. Only gradually do they unfold their full effect, sharpening our perceptions and enhancing the commonplace, showing us a promising route for airport architecture of the future midway between banality and pathos.

The grounding of the Swiss national airline Swissair meant that upon its completion, the dock remained empty for nearly a year—an abandoned building stranded like a whale on the open tarmac, to be seen only from afar through the binoculars of devoted planespotters.

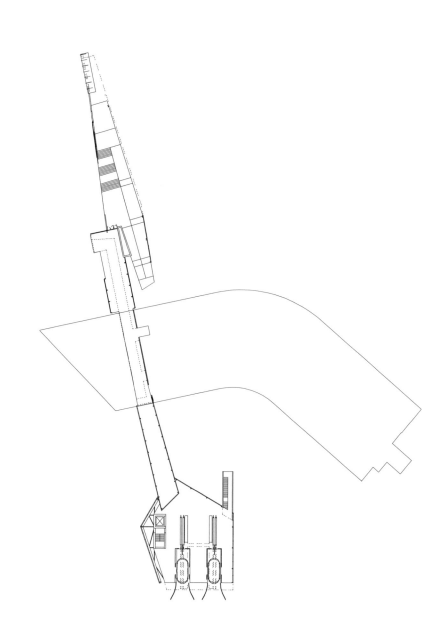

IN THE AIR

DENISE BRATTON

The scheme for a pivotal piece of urban infrastructure in Portland—a city dedicated to enlightened public transportation and sustainability—was designed to advance a redevelopment project that would also guarantee the survival of an economic and historic institutional "anchor": the Marquam Hill campus of the Oregon Health & Science University (OHSU). Overlooking the Willamette River, Marquam Hill dominates Portland's cityscape. When real-estate magnate and transportation pioneer Philip Augustus Marquam arrived there during the California Gold Rush, he found a city of 1,000 inhabitants which in the meantime has grown into a million-strong metropolitan region. In 1857, Marquam, who by then was the largest landowner of his time, purchased 300 acres of hilltop land for $2,500. The rail transportation hub he later envisioned was defeated only by the topographical limitations of the site. It would be more than 150 years before technology—in this case, an aerial tramway—would catch up with his vision.

In 1981, a loose consortium of diverse academic research institutions and healthcare facilities that had evolved over more than a century were brought together to create OHSU, which today dominates Portland as its single largest employer. When, in 1999, it became clear that the main campus on Marquam Hill had reached its limits in terms of space and transportation infrastructure, the institution's future became a public issue. Various schemes for expansion were studied, the most viable involving a tract of some 35 acres on Portland's South Waterfront. Ultimately, OHSU partnered with the municipality and private developers to come up with what is considered an "elegant solution" that projects the city's future in longer terms. The mise-en-scène was now set for a twenty-first-century infrastructural move that would link the hilltop and waterfront campuses, and at the same time activate physically disconnected parts of the city. After considering a gondola-type lift, a tunnel, a funicular, and a monorail, the bold move to install an aerial tramway was launched. Dismissed early in the process as a "castle in the air," it is only the second one to be built in the United States.

The project led to Portland's first international architectural competition based on the logic that the tramway would be embraced by the public "because it would be well designed." A brief was announced in 2002, when the City of Portland and the non-profit Portland Aerial Transportation, Inc. (PATI) hired Reed Kroloff to manage the competition and to make it as transparent to the public as possible. In January 2003, the field was narrowed from sixteen to four firms. Each was invited to submit design proposals and address the city in a public presentation. Portland's *Oregonian* followed the process closely with reportage and editorials. When the jury met to make the final selection, the public was invited. Several hundred took advantage of the opportunity and the auditorium was full. Each firm's presentation was podcast on the web. Citizens at every level of society were informed, and were curious about the outcome. Public participation is common in Switzerland, but unusual in the United States. The jury unanimously named agps the winner of the competition.

The firm's scheme was grounded in the basic idea of a light, connective infrastructure built with a strict economy of means. The tram
was not to touch the hospital at the upper station, and it could only tread
lightly on the urban fabric descending the hill. It was therefore conceived as if there were *no site at all*, as a light and ethereal superstructure that seems to dematerialize, touching earth with three light foot-
prints: the upper station, an intermediate tower, and the lower station.
Two "reflective" cable cars would carry passengers up and down. On
the other hand, the design was approached as if all of Portland were the
site for a viewing machine from which the city could be seen in ways
it had never been seen before, and the tram itself could be seen from
everywhere.

Wary of the fact that in some quarters (including the mayor's office) the tram was preconceived as an urban "icon," the agps architects
went in the opposite direction with their winning proposal. They
stressed the tram's connective and infrastructural functions rather than
its presence as architectural object. They enlarged the concept of the
"machine for moving people" to include other objectives linking the
tram to the rest of the city: the *green connection* proposed the creation
of a new park along a restored watershed; the *land connection* proposed
a bridge crossing the freeway as well as a series of pedestrian and cycle
paths traversing the hillside; and the *aerial connection*, the centerpiece,
physically joined two parts of the city as well as providing a visual link
between the city and Mt. Hood in the distance.

The design of the bicable tramway was a high-stakes proposition.
Its three "pieces" were enormous in scale since the loads each would
have to bear were tremendous, and the tolerances for the placement of
elements like the track cables at each of the stations were close to zero.
The upper station was conceived as an open, freestanding platform clad
in an expanded metal skin that folds and drapes over the station to let
in light and air. A vertical cantilevered assembly standing 140 feet above

ground, the station platform is supported on braced-steel legs that barely clear the street and parking garage below. It was built to resist a later-
al force of around a million pounds from the cables carrying the tramcars. Housed inside the reflective silver structure is the counterweight,
hued a brilliant yellow-green, gleaming from beneath the platform. Projecting out behind this, the fire stair painted bright red is easy to spot
in an emergency. Passengers reach and board the tram at the ninth floor
of OHSU's new Patient Care Facility via a bridge that connects the station with the hospital. The two are structurally independent to ensure
that the forces to which the station is regularly subjected do not trans-
fer to its neighbor and cause even the slightest vibration.

The intermediate support tower midway down the hillside was designed to respond to the physical forces that act upon it and to allow the
tramcar leaving the lower station to achieve lift-off quickly so as to clear
the highway. Constructed of hollow steel plate reinforced with T-stiff-
eners and concrete, it rises to 200 feet, its broad shaft footed on the hillside, tapered to make room for the tramcars to pass, flaring out again to
brace the technical saddles, and leaning in to meet the tram cables at a
90-degree angle. The lower station, like the upper one, is open to its surroundings, but framed by expanded metal, making a material connection between departure and arrival. The tram operators work in a control room on the floor above, while a machine room one floor below
contains all the technical equipment. The housing for the
tram cables dramatically cuts through the space of the station, dwarfing passengers entering and leaving.

The two sleek, pod-like tramcars were built by Gan-
gloff in Bern, Switzerland, makers of Lamborghini auto
bodies, without the aid of computer integrated manufacturing. Hand-making turned out to be the most efficient fabrication option and two elderly craftsmen returned from re-
tirement to do the job. The aluminum and glass cars glisten

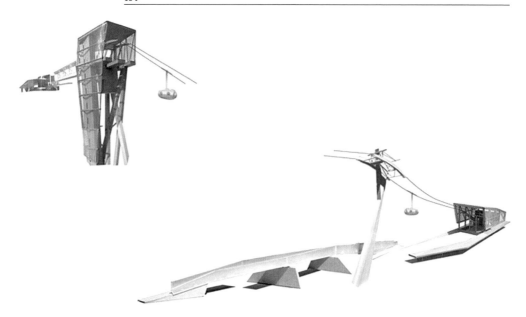

and in certain lighting conditions literally dematerialize against the sky over Portland. Their lighter-than-air appearance defies their actual weight of twelve tons each.

Considerable mystery surrounded PATI's funding projections right from the beginning. In a first meeting with the clients, agps ran aground on what turned out to be a budget based on "thin air" rather than research. No technical data whatsoever had been analyzed. Not wanting to let the matter proceed any further without drawing a line under what they considered a purely "conceptual" phase of the budget, agps informed the project managers that the tram could not be built for the "abstract" figure originally proposed. One of the architects spontaneously picked up a paper and sketched out a "cost diagram" anticipating a budget of $40 to $45 million; he then pocketed the napkin, and the managers said they would "handle it." The whole process was thus left up in the air and there was speculation in the office that the project might be abandoned.

In fact, the budget went to $47 million, which is not such a huge sum given that the tramway was envisioned as the key that would unlock the potential of a $30 billion development scheme being pursued by the city and South Waterfront developers. And despite the vicissitudes of the political stakes, budget projections, public opinion, architects' reputations, and media intervention, the tramway was built. The architects were stalwart in the face of repeated cost-cutting demands from managers who came in and then left the project like children playing musical chairs. At some point, however, when the cost cuts verged on the dangerous, the architects realized that they were the last people left standing, so to speak, and that as the only ones who had been on the project from the beginning, it was their responsibility to call a halt to the cost-cutting. Additional funds were found.

By the time the tram opened to the public, five managers had rotated into (and out of) the mix. With a budget that continued to be squeezed right up to completion, construction was harrowing. Detailing had to be sacrificed. Even more serious, the derogatory phrase "castle in the air" came to haunt the architects, who found themselves literally "building in the air" with no physical access to the site during construction. An underlying problem was that the construction crews were working with imperial measurements typical of North America, while the tram machinery was fabricated in metric. Alert to the difficulty of meeting zero tolerances given the inevitable fractional variances between the two systems, one of the architects raised the specter of NASA's Mars Climate Orbiter, which was destroyed in 1999 due to just such a minor discrepancy in measurements: the spacecraft flew too close to the planet and was incinerated by atmospheric stress and friction. The architect's warning went unheeded, but fortunately there were no negative consequences.

The silvery tramcars, like the central mast of the superstructure itself, arrived in Portland on giant barges. Both were laboriously installed with colossal cranes requiring the kind of logistic scenario planning that one imagines to be the purview of blockbuster disaster movies. It must be mentioned that although the scale of infrastructure required to transport and install the enormous components of the tramway stretches the limits of our comprehension, the whole operation begets other, potentially larger (even if unseen) forms of infrastructure of an economic, technical, logistical, and administrative kind. Not only does architecture at this level exceed its own bounds to become *infrastructure*, but infrastructure on this scale depends on an ever-expanding array of systems, each of which possesses its own *architecture* and logic.

The tramcars can carry up to eighty passengers each, traveling a distance of 3,300 feet between stations. Dropping 500 feet

from hill to waterfront, this is a three-minute ride each way. The tramway opened to OHSU employees on December 1, 2006, and to the public less than a month later. Reception was positive, not least because of
a dramatic incident while the tramway was still under construction:
a young boy scheduled for a kidney transplant on Marquam Hill was
prevented from reaching the hospital by a severe ice storm that paralyzed Portland, rendering all roads unsafe. Waiving tremendous red
tape, OHSU officials sent the boy up the hill by tram and his crucial operation took place on schedule. At times, the real purpose and import
of urban infrastructure is made concrete in the public's mind; this was
one of those times. Little more than ten months after it opened, the
tramway carried its millionth passenger: its ultimate utility has been
amply demonstrated. Not surprisingly, a certain glamour and even an
iconic character did indeed accrue to this steely, light-footed urban mar-
vel as it quickly inserted itself into the collective imagination of the city.

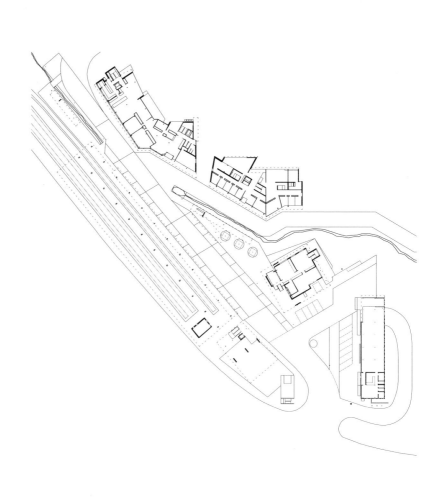

ON THE EDGE

VERENA DOERFLER

Busses pull up and spew out groups of people. The groups split up into even smaller clusters: some head off to the shop, some to the post office; still others set off for the train station where they board trains. And once the doors have closed behind them and the train has left the station, only silence remains.

A car turns a corner and comes to a halt in a space in the designated parking lot. A man armed with shopping bags of all sorts gets out of the car, locks the doors, and sets off for the shop. He goes inside. Again, only silence remains.

These long-drawn-out silences can get to city people after a while. Even more so the empty space—it is as if there had never been anything here at all, as if this were the end of the world, the outskirts of a rural nowhere. But then the next bus arrives, or a car, or an elderly woman who takes up her post at the bus shelter across from the train station—and waits.

Rural space means emptiness, or at least it seems as if it was once that way. "Uncontrolled development" is the term the experts use to describe the meandering assortment of residential structures now laying claim to rural landscapes the world over. What was once a village—a concentrated center—is now just an area sprawled out over the countryside, its limits in constant need of redefinition. The result is a vacuum. The center cannot hold. Age-old boundaries give way. And then there are these empty spaces, social as well as spatial voids. A sustainability horror scenario.

Rural agglomerations are particularly susceptible to these processes. They are neither village nor city, but rather intermediate spaces—a gap between urban density and unchecked rural development. Esslingen has also become just such an in between space. A village now firmly embedded in Zurich's affluent outskirts in the Pfannenstiel Hills midway between Greifensee Lake and Lake Zurich, Esslingen is currently home to 1,569 residents, many of whom came here in search of rural tranquility and an easy commute to Zurich and the surrounding region. More and more living space was created to meet the demand—a development which more or less agrees with the area's original inhabitants. Not surprisingly, the result is a textbook case of uncontrolled rural development.

Or would be, were it not for the Esslinger Dreieck and with it a strategy to tackle decades of unraveling social and spatial relationships with an architectural counterpoint. The Dreieck is a new center situated in the middle of the village at the place where Esslingerstrasse, Forchstrasse, and Oetwilstrasse come together to form a triangle. It is a place where the regular theater of coming and going, movement and stillness, temporary fullness and complete emptiness can be observed. It was also the very first architectural project undertaken by agps, meaning that both concept and implementation now lie a good twenty years in the past.

Yet at first glance, Esslinger Dreieck still looks a bit new, as if it had not yet completely arrived in the present, as if it had not yet come to terms with itself. This has nothing at all to do with the architecture, though it may have to do with another factor that makes rural space what it is today: a space in which time flows differently, in which changes have an architectural half-life that is twice or even three times as long as it would be in an urban environment. Sitting at the heart of the Esslinger Dreieck, which includes a bus and train station, a post office, a village shop, a Park & Ride garage, commercial buildings, and green spaces, is like sitting in a place which somehow manages to unite past, present, and future, or which is still appropriating all three of them for itself.

It could scarcely be claimed that the architecture here just came in and took control of the surroundings, conquering, or even occupying it with sweeping gestures in the way that so many of today's monumental constructions do. On the contrary. The architects did something that was unheard of in Esslingen in those days: they took what they saw and then took it a step further.

They planned and built a centralizing architecture, an architecture capable of pulling things together which fitted into the existing landscape, topography, and settlement structure like a piece of a puzzle that had been missing all along. They were driven by the need to prevent the melting away of social and spatial structures by lending them new shape, and were guided in this by one of the most defining—and fluid—features of the whole area, namely by the "Chnolibach," a creek that winds its way through the center of the village.

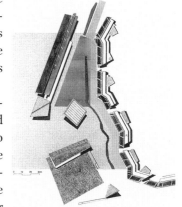

This wonderful little stream lends direction to the entire architectural arrangement. It is a natural artifact around which the structures unfold. The creek divides the site into two mutually influential parts. One side is a public space which plays with the very idea of openness and whose free-standing buildings—train station, post office, and village store—enter into a dialogue with one another. On the other

side of the creek is a series of office buildings arranged in a row. Their floor plans—and this is another key aspect of the concept—interact with the geometry of the flowing stream and add volume to the space. Their south facades, which face the public space, form a nearly contiguous body that is visually reminiscent of something best described as a "wall": a wall of architecture intended not only as a noise barrier for the planned residential units in the northern part of the site, but also as a wall behind which future residents in search of privacy can withdraw.

However, the one element that attracts the most attention in this meticulously coordinated architectural composition is the terminal station of the Forch railway line—the locals refer to it as their "Aunt Frieda." The need for a new railway station was what sparked the search for a new architectural concept in the first place. The railway originally ran along the northeastern side of the triangle, along Usterstrasse, the village's main thoroughfare, which it shared with both heavy automobile traffic and local children cycling to and from school. In the late 1980s, the close proximity of children and cars resulted in a fatality and officials decided it was high time to rectify the situation. The railway would run along the southwestern boundary of the triangle and the last station on the line would be built on the road to the village of Forch. And thus the Esslinger Dreieck was born.

Now the "flying roofs" atop the station's "light"—in both senses of the word—steel frame point the way to the public space, could even be said to serve as a kind of open "curtain" on daily life, or at least on the daily life that takes place here.

When busses arrive at the transportation hub, passengers switch from train to bus or vice versa, or take the opportunity to do a little shopping for their daily needs—in the village shop diagonally opposite the train station, for example, whose pure rectangular geometry represents the exact opposite of the station's open and airy architecture (which in winter can be a bit chilly for those waiting for a train). The shop with its long and somewhat low concrete-slab facade serves as a boundary between the public space above and the lower level where there is a green space and the entrance to the free Park & Ride garage. As a result of the interplay between these two levels, the shop is transformed into a kind of suspended object—and into an instructive case study in statics. This is because it is the weight of the solid slabs of concrete on the building's southern side that allows the structure to hang

a few meters out over the drop in the terrain, despite its "light" steel frame. The resulting overhang provides a generous entrance to the parking garage situated below.

Advanced construction techniques in other words. The village chronicles tell of the hordes of architecture students who back in 1999, after construction was completed, came to pay their respects to Esslingen's famed "swimming and flying" village store. Or as one of Esslingen's long-time residents put it: "They all just came and took their pictures and were amazed. It was a building designed by architects in America—it had to be like that."

Then there is the post office set between the train station, shop, and the office buildings, the virtual fulcrum in the overall design of the triangle. It is a small, cube-shaped structure that serves as the connecting element between the two sides of the entire site. To sum it up, it is a wonderfully practical little cube. The post office was also given a flying roof echoing that atop the train station.

Turning our backs on the public space, a generous and contemporary version of the traditional village square with all its inherent functions, our attention is caught by the virtual wall of the office buildings on the left, which was to have led to the private residential space beyond.

But to this day the wall is still waiting for the residential units to be built. Shrinking back from the new, especially when money is concerned, seems to be a fact of human nature. Or at least is a trait that is clearly not unknown to investors. Nonetheless, this (conceptual) crossover between the public and the private halves of the Esslinger Dreieck and the wall formed by the office buildings is where the two main conceptual elements meet: public sphere and private sphere, variety and density. The two office buildings which have already been constructed—and are occupied by the consulting engineers Basler & Hofmann and owned by the real estate company Rehalp AG, which was the principal interest behind the entire Esslinger Dreieck—have already accomplished what was originally set out in the 1989 call for bids: the blending of private and public functional units.

The floor plans of the office buildings with their open facades facing south and nested in the angular geometry laid out by the stream are representative of building concepts which although common today were completely new when they were originally conceived: small glassed-in individual offices combined with shared offices and a ground-floor cafeteria that serves as both conference room and communal space for the company. The crossover between public and private takes place right here in the intermediate space of the company's own building. This was long before other companies began to adopt similar philosophies for their own offices. Not only is there a large amount of glass along the building's northern facade, which from this perspective lends it a great deal of transparency and lightness, but there is also an impressive terrace area—the envy of all who see it—that serves as an alternative workspace for company employees. The fact that the locals sometimes refer to them as "the ones from Basler & Hofmann" who "take up all the parking space in the public garage," and that they tend to be described as the "strangers" who otherwise have little to do with village life is proof of the following: that we here in Esslingen, like just about any other rural community, live in a kind of time warp in which all changes—as stated before—are subject to different sets of temporal laws.

Last but not least, the Esslinger Dreieck can also claim to have been one of the first to experiment with ecological forms of building and planning long before it became fashionable, and long before sustainability had become the *sine qua non* of forward-looking construction. The client expressed a wish for the "use of solar energy," and agps responded with an entire palette of environmentally sound construction techniques, including insulating materials made of renewable resources, photovoltaic systems, solar panels, heat pump water heaters, horizontal loops, cross-ventilation techniques, and the installation of woodchip-fired heating systems for all of the structures. And oh how happy the clients were to hear of such innovation, such visions of the future!

But to return to the beginning: Sitting at the Esslinger Dreieck, you might feel like a visitor to another space in time. Aware of your surroundings' past, you discover the future in the architecture, and look for the present in what is happening all around you: in the changes that come and go, the alternation between fullness and emptiness, the interplay of appropriation and a slight sense of alienation. It will take some time before the Esslinger Dreieck truly becomes the center of the village; perhaps only the next generation will accept it as such. Now it is just "modern," maybe even "futuristic." Getting used to it takes

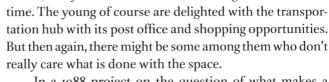

time. The young of course are delighted with the transportation hub with its post office and shopping opportunities. But then again, there might be some among them who don't really care what is done with the space.

In a 1988 project on the question of what makes a "good place," the author wrote: "Acceptance is not handed to you on a plate. Effort is just as much a fundamental aspect of acceptance as seeking out new frontiers is a fundamental aspect of the imagination."

Nothing more remains to be said.

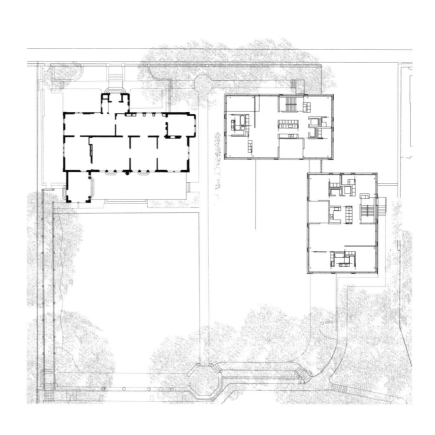

THE SPHINX WITHOUT A SECRET

BENJAMIN MUSCHG

The childless miller decided that the time had come to name his successor. He set his three apprentices a task: they were to go forth, and the one who brought him the best horse would inherit his mill. Little Hans knew no better than to serve a cat for seven years who had promised him an exceptionally fine horse. In the end he even built the cat a house made of silver. But foolishness is no hindrance to making something of one's life in Grimm's fairy tales. Hans did not receive the mill, but he did end up marrying the cat, who in the meantime had been transformed into a princess. Together with her, he lived in the palace that had once been the silver house and spent the rest of his days as a wealthy man.

In the mid-nineteenth century, Friedrich Wegmann left Würglen, his uncle's mill in the Zurich Oberland, to seek his fortune. After serving as an apprentice and journeyman in France and Italy he returned to Zurich in 1870, where, like the poor miller's boy in the famed fairy tale published twenty years before his birth, he soon acquired all the wealth he would ever need. He built his own palace in the form of

Villa Hohenbühl, a splendid mansion on a vine-covered hill beyond the old city walls. Wegmann had not met a cat on his travels, but he had invented the roller mill, a method of grinding corn that heralded the end of the millstone era and the industrialization of milling worldwide.

Wegmann built his new home in the style of a majestic Italian villa above the Baroque estate of Kreuzbühl in 1889. The main building was designed by Alfred Friedrich Bluntschli, a student of Semper, while the garden sloping steeply towards what is now Stadelhofen train station was landscaped by Evariste Mertens. In the 1920s, Wegmann's son Gustav had the estate enlarged by commissioning the architect Otto Honegger with a new, but smaller villa, and Evariste's sons Walter and Oskar with a new park. The most recent—and probably the last—addition to the ensemble came in 2004 with the construction of two pavil-

ion-style apartment blocks. The artist Blanca Blarer joined forces with agps to produce a design inspired by an Andy Warhol quotation: it is "a place to think silver."

Situated on a peaceful, south-facing hillside overlooking the lake with Stadelhofen train station at its foot and at the heart of Zurich's triangle of highbrow culture marked out by the opera house, theater, and art gallery, the site would indeed make an ideal kingdom for a silver palace. The L-shaped lot adjoins Honegger's historicist faced concrete building, which enjoys listed status as evidence of the antimodernist tendencies in early modernism. Yet it is missing one key component for the kind of architectural splendor that would allow foolish Hans and his princess to live happily ever after: space. Perhaps the two apartment buildings on Hohenbühlstrasse are an example of how architectural grandeur can also be an illusion.

Enthroned on their plinths as if they had just settled down for a picnic in this exceptionally secluded spot, the two shiny, silver cubes are curiously close to one other and yet far removed from the world around them. On the side facing the street, what seem to be the rear sides of the two buildings project out over a small courtyard where you could equally imagine a horse and cart driving up or a UFO landing. That the grand entrance might be ruined by a couple of rusty bikes, despite the sign requesting that two-wheelers be left in front of the wall, is much harder to imagine. The courtyard is carved out of the property's natural stone wall and bordered by semi-transparent glass that gives the merest hint of a better world within. Think silver, think luxury. And both can be glimpsed at the point between the two buildings where the residents' privacy is assured not by glass, but by a row of white concrete stelae. Behind this is the garage, the grandest room of all.

Although garages are the entrance halls of the twenty-first century, they are still largely ignored as an architectural theme. In several previous projects agps had already taken into account the fact that modern citizens often enter their residences by car. Neither the Trüb House in Horgen nor the Kormann-Stüber House in Küsnacht 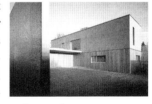 make a hierarchical distinction between entrance areas, for example, and when the Waschanstalt in Wollishofen was converted, a slight gradient was used to provide the semi-subterranean garage with natural light. The Hohenbühl blocks took this idea a stage further: you enter your luxurious house in your luxurious car through a luxurious entrance. Instead of getting out of your car in a basement that smell of fumes, you alight into a space filled with natural light and air and visually connected to both the inside and the outside.

The stelae filtering the visual relationships from the inside out and vice versa do not shield the four-wheeled treasures within from scrutiny; in fact they positively invite it. agps first had the idea of obscuring automobiles behind vertical blinds for a General Motors exhibition pavilion back in 1996. However, the American motor company was not convinced that hiding its goods would make them more appealing. In a 2002 competition for Stuttgart's Mercedes-Benz-Museum, agps used a similar structure made of silver vertical lamellas as a way of experimenting with ways of steering visual correlations and exploring

the theme of camouflage in the luxury sector, which in the entrance hall of the contemporaneous Hohenbühl project was to conceal far more than just glossy silver limousines.

The two cubes are offset from one another and each contains three family-friendly apartments, one per story. Each apartment is a reasonable size without being excessive (just under 2,000 square feet of floor space and four bedrooms), the floor plans are well thought out and use the space well, the materials are simple yet sophisticated, and there is a lockable loggia but no private external garden space. The building could pass as social housing for the wealthy if its three-layered facade did not create the illusion of a truly luxurious construction.

Large wall elements on the inside, ceiling-to-floor windows in the middle, and chromium steel mesh screens on the outside providing security and protection from the sun form three separate layers running round the whole building and can be moved in relation to each other to vary both internal and external perceptions. The luxurious nature of the facade is conveyed less by the promise of unlimited power over the relationship between the world inside and the world outside than by the splendor of its appearance. The electrically operated silver lamellar drapes interact with the layered facade underneath and alter their appearance according to how far they are opened, the time of day, and the season: they can seem smooth or bulky, diaphanous or impenetrable, colorful or metallic gray.

The wire mesh normally used in industrial bakeries gives this third and final development of the Wegmann property the sublime appearance it needs to hold its own in such prestigious company. Yet it could also be interpreted as an unintentional homage to that Swiss pioneer of the grain processing industry who settled here in the late nineteenth century.

The reverence shown to the American pioneer of Pop Art, on the other hand, is entirely intentional. Warhol reputedly described himself as deeply superficial, a characteristic best reflected by his fixation on all things silver.

Warhol's famous Factory on New York's 47th Street, where between 1963 and 1967 he was visited by a motley collection of fashionable New York types, was completely clad in silver foil and painted silver. The obsession was to haunt Warhol in macabre fashion even at his darkest moment in 1968, when radical feminist Valerie Solanas shot him with three bullets that, so the story goes, she had painted silver in the belief that he was a vampire. Truman Capote probably came closer to the truth about Warhol when he described him as a sphinx without a secret.

And there can be no more appropriate description of these residential blocks on Hohenbühlstrasse in Zurich. Hiding behind the buildings' mysteriously beautiful veil is utterly unspectacular architecture for everyday life.

Yet as the secret we imagine behind the sphinx's visage is revealed ever more patently to be an illusion, the stronger we believe in its existence. Nothing is more contradictory, more puzzling, and hence more interesting than "The Sphinx Without a Secret," the short story by Oscar Wilde from which Truman Capote's description of Andy Warhol is taken. In Wilde's tale, Lord Murchison drives his lover to her death with his suspicions about her mysterious secret. He later discovers that she merely liked the idea of mystery, and that there was no great secret at all. The story ends with him opening his morocco case containing her photo and saying: "I wonder?"

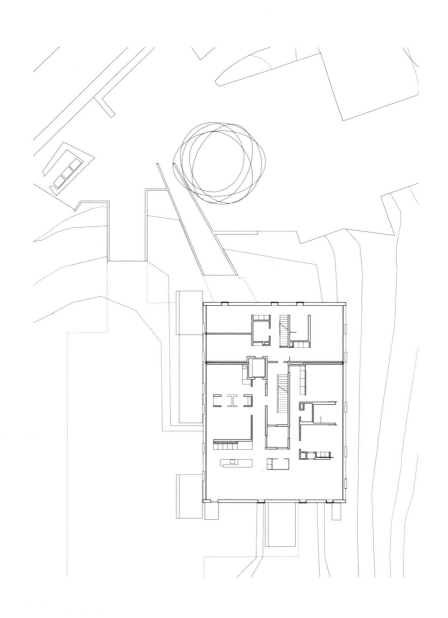

MIMICRY

CLAUDE ENDERLE

The view is superb. As the cloud clears on this early summer day, a vista emerges of the main basin of Lake Zurich to the north, of the lakeshore to the east, and of the Obersee or upper lake to the south. Beyond that, barely discernible on the horizon, is the gray mass of the Alps with their jagged contours. Surely there must be a postcard of the view from Kilchberg.

I am enjoying this expansive, unobstructed view from the terrace of a loft on the southern edge of the village. The open veranda with its deserted deckchair recalls days of carefree idleness as well as the black-and-white architecture photography of the 1930s—images showing the seductive poses of the ostentatiously indolent such as might have accompanied writings about what the Bauhaus celebrated as "liberated living," although the residential architecture of that era has precious little in common with today's. The parapets along both the longer eastern side of the terrace and the shorter southern side are glazed. The glass facade of the eastern side of the building affords views into three of the rooms inside: a bathroom at the back, next to it a dressing room with built-in closets, and at the front a bedroom. Except that these are not really three separate rooms at all, since the floor-to-ceiling connecting walls are actually sliding doors that allow the rooms to be opened or closed off at will, thus emphasizing their arrangement as a suite along the facade.

Every second element in the glass facade can be opened, allowing each room to be extended outward if desired and reinforcing the idea of an enfilade: a suite of rooms arranged orthogonally to an accentuated longitudinal axis. The open-plan concept continues into the living room I enter upon returning from the terrace. This room is not strictly separated from the bedroom either: exterior and interior are connected by a fireplace with a stone bench, and in the foreground a suite of chairs grouped around it. Beyond this, the living room extends back along the entire length of the building, opening up an uninterrupted view of the dining area and kitchen at the back. The kitchen has two parallel rows of kitchen units and strip windows belonging to the west facade. The kitchen units and fireplace face one another, further accentuating the longitudinal orientation of the living room along the south facade. The openings on this side are economical, if not to say modest in both number and size, and offer selected views of the outside. Yet they are not picture windows as such. The leafy view of the park seen from the dining table and kitchen through the strip windows facing west provides a refreshing contrast to these rather restricted lookouts. The only irritating factor is a familiar view of Lake Zurich that seems almost to intrude between the trees. Only at second glance do you realize there is a mirror covering a roughly three-foot-wide section of the window on the inside of the facade element. Yet even knowing there is a mirror there, it is impossible to escape this optical illusion entirely—there are just too many horizons trying to connect.

The mirror trick serves to counteract the readability of the architecture, or what one might call the rather spartan orderliness of the floor plan. For only when seen in its compressed mirror image does the light well emerge as the true, all-illuminating center of the apartment. The floor-to-ceiling glass paneling that joins it to the fireplace bench invites a glimpse into the bedroom opposite with the lake in the background, another diagonally across to the stairwell, and another down below. Like in a hall of mirrors, by shifting my position slightly and looking to the left I can see two things at once that would not normally be visible at the same time: the stairwell and front door seen from the outside together with the inside of the entrance hall. If I were to move a little further to the left and open the first of the sliding doors, I would be able to make a spatial connection  between the kitchen and the hall; and if I then opened another sliding door, I would not only make the small office vanish as a room in its own right, but would also open up the view of the western terrace and the park beyond … and so on and so forth. As the reader may already have guessed, the trick of opening, half opening or closing windows and sliding doors opens up a seemingly endless variety of views, at the same time revealing ever new aspects (in both senses of the word) of the apartment.

Yet the apartment is not really as endless as all that, even after including the options for expanding it to the north. And what at first sight seems to be a rather spartan floor plan on closer inspection turns out to be variations on a theme. In keeping with the times, the notion of contingency seems to be the architectural leitmotif here with rooms that offer a range of possibilities to the imaginative resident. The austere stairwell with its black steel staircase, the concrete walls, and the play of bluish green light created by the mingling of direct and reflected sunlight in the light well takes me back down to the ground floor. The sharp contrast between the dark shadows and gleaming white paving at the bottom of the light well recalls modern photographs of details of Japanese architecture, in which harsh light and cool colors highlight the precision of the transitions between glass, steel, and stone. So why do I keep thinking of seaweed? Is that what makes this image so exotic—beyond the actual subject?

Only after arriving downstairs do I realize that the spatial concept at the northern end of the building is completely different. The two duplexes on this side of the building have hardly any sliding doors. So does that mean the space is organized less flexibly? No, but the flexibility here is achieved in a completely different way: through the exciting interaction of spatial opposites, of clearly defined functional spaces at the micro level and apparently unlimited living space at the macro level, whose function can be changed by rearranging the furniture, thus once again endowing the apartment with many different aspects. Looking back at the building from the forecourt, the entrance and windows look as if scattered capriciously across the north facade. Smooth as glass, thin as a wafer, and broadly framed, they are like pasted-on postage stamps. And what about the east facade? From this vantage point at least, it, too, looks as if it were bolted on. The boxes for the roller shutters are integrated into the rendered parapets so that it looks as if the glazing continues underneath them. What the "randomly" placed mirror elements on the strip windows did upstairs on the inside, they do here on the outside: they make for confusion.

Standing out as features in their own right rather than as part of a larger whole, these silver-gray facade elements in Canadian pine relate a narrative of their own in front of the strip glazing and matching rendering. Fluidly cascading downward they effortlessly even out the differences in depth between the parapets and strip windows. Are they allusions to historic architectural elements? Or are they a continuation of the visual message communicated by the postage-stamp windows:

fitted elements as material images? Whatever the case, I like the textile-
like quality of these elements whose assorted colors suggest an exercise
in camouflage, a coquettish accentuation of their formal otherness.
In the forecourt with a weeping willow—what a wonderful closing
metaphor!—I am standing in front of two wedge-shaped concrete aisles.
One leads to the entrance, the other to the parking garage, thus placing
humans and machines on a par. So the hill as high as the top floor flank-
ing the western side of this gray monolith is the parking garage! Meanwhile, the eastern side facing the lake with its three stories of strip glazing stands proudly at the top of a slope, forcing observers at the foot of
the hill to crane their neck and look up as if learning the meaning of
the word monumental for the first time. The lower portion of the west
facade—which formally echoes the east—disappears into the ground.
So what we have here are the clear contours of a cube with horizontal
strip windows set in a generously dimensioned green space—a nod to
the black-and-white photography of early modernist residential architecture perhaps?

No. Viewed from the street in bright sunlight, the grain of the rendering on the south facade is unmistakable. The effect of the stuck-on
postage-stamp windows is repeated here, too, until suddenly, without
any material forewarning, an unframed door to the garden appears.
A camouflaged door on the outside? What a quirky idea! That reminds
me of the image of a Baroque…

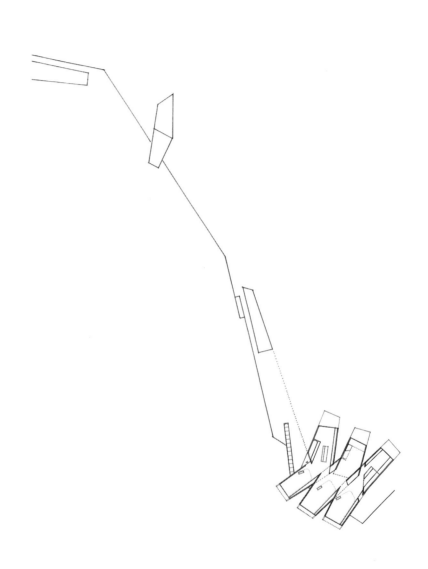

HOUSE FOR TRINOCULAR VIEWING

DENISE BRATTON

Topanga Ranch, site of agps's second residence in the same canyon and for the same client, presented itself as an expanded context for its ongoing investigation of the notion of "house." The rationale for building on undeveloped canyon land was part of a process that evolved over time. The story began with the idea of building the first house—Topanga I—as an investment. As the project evolved, the clients formed a personal attachment that made it impossible for them to treat Topanga I as a "spec house." After adopting it as a "weekend house," they reversed their long-held opposition to living at a remove from the city and committed to making it their "home." This progression implicated the clients in a larger revolution that seems to be afoot: the abandonment of cities in favor of rural living verging on the utopian. Commissioning a house in semi-wild territory transcended mere property development or even home-building *stricto senso*: it quickly became a matter of infrastructure as placemaking.

As urban infrastructure deteriorates and cannot be updated fast enough to serve the needs of growing and densifying cities, and as the

specter of infrastructural insecurity (once a condition exclusive to the developing world) becomes a fact of American life, too, the private water well and septic tank, and the technology needed to capture solar energy take on new appeal. But there are lethal threats to rural life in California, the most prominent of which are drought and wildfires. Imagine the scene: a cement pad lying empty amid the densely overgrown chaparral of rural Topanga Canyon, six miles inland from the Pacific coast just south of Malibu. The house that once rested on the pad fell victim to the Old Topanga Fire that swept through the canyon in November 1993. The ranch to which it belonged was abandoned and left languishing on the real estate market until the architects, along with their clients Stewart Middler and Antoinette Hubenette, circled the wagons and determined to develop the property and build a second house.

Middler and Hubenette may at first have been daunted by the legacy of the dwelling that burned to the ground not far from their first house, and perhaps also by the new strict grading and fire safety requirements imposed by the city. Having moved somewhat cautiously into their role as patrons of innovative architecture, these clients were in no rush. After all, they already had a house. It was aging well, gradually being assimilated into the natural landscape to the point that it could hardly be seen from the empty pad across the road. But there was no denying the breathtaking views from the promontory of the new site. For their part, the architects were inspired by the rigorous challenges it posed.

A hasty sketch drawn on a paper tablecloth in a Zurich restaurant marks the moment that the second Topanga House was conceived and another experiment in dwelling began to take shape. Unlike the Hollywood House, where the problem was to "nick" a house into a very tight parcel of land where city and country meet but that is still *in* the city, the Topanga Ranch presented an entirely new scenario on a new scale: a remote property, topographically quite diverse, reachable only by a disturbingly long access road, but graced by an independent source of water and full, 360-degree exposure to sun, moon, and stars—essentially ten acres of pure view.

Analyzing the site and its topography, a vast expanse of rolling hills marked by broad plateaus and narrow paths, the architects read in the plateaus the smooth form of a dolphin's back, whereas the paths snaking round and through the hills took on a more serpentine aspect. The "dolphin-like" zones were identified as potential building sites that could be programmed for dwelling or any number of rural-agricultural purposes: corralling horses and other animals, gardening, fruit-growing, beekeeping, composting, water pumping, renewable energy generation, storage—all the functions related to sustainable living "off the grid." The paths were seen as lines connecting these functions and thus transforming the site into a unified *place*. The long road leading to the abandoned cement pad, existing circulation routes, retaining walls, and other vague traces of movement were all carefully considered as an internal system of connections.

Site planning elicited a utopian vision before any serious thought was given to building per se. Questions of exposure and orientation, soil quality, and access to water across the whole site determined which zones would lend themselves to dwelling, growing, husbandry, irrigation, fire prevention, energy generation, and waste management—the basic permaculture. Once this was established, the architects decided that the leftover and marginal landscape would remain untouched. The arid Mediterranean climate of the canyon suggested drought-resistant planting, but even this was strictly regulated in view of the omnipresent threat of fire. The rising cost of water and impending restrictions on its

use were also disincentives to introducing any more plant material than was absolutely essential to bring the vision for this site into focus.

Dubbing their approach "gentle intervention," the architects embraced the whole spectrum of life on the site rather than any single element when they returned to the problem of where to situate the house itself. There was agreement all round that the new house should be built where the former one had stood, but the act of designing the second Topanga House was spurred by another project of around the same time. This was the exhibition "Latent Utopias: Experiments within Contemporary Architecture" at the Landesmuseum Joanneum in Graz in 2002–2003. The statement accompanying the agps installation emphasized that "architectural formations evolve from a network of relationships in a state of continuous re-definition." The playful exploration of novel kinds of space started with simple, origami-like experiments leading to the production of extended volumes roughly modeled in folded paper, which were then combined, recombined, and bundled in a study of extended and bent tubular forms. These were bifurcated and interconnected at crucial junctures. For Graz, this experimentation culminated in an inflatable model constructed of translucent latex—a rubber "skin" filled with helium. The resemblance to personal flotation devices designed by Leonardo da Vinci was startling.

Building on the formal results of the Graz experiments, the house for Topanga Ranch was conceived as three hollow, tubular structures glazed at both ends and "bundled" together, connecting at strategic junctures, which the architects began to think of as "tangential intersections," where the tubes overlap and each appears to branch off into another. The house that emerged obeys neither a modernist open plan nor a sequence of rooms in the traditional sense. It is conceived on two levels that straddle a sloping plateau, resting on a retaining wall that seems to belong to the earth. The lower level discreetly contains the mechanical systems and service rooms, mysteriously disappearing into the ground and becoming one with the level of the main entrance from the north. Three cantilevered "habitable tubes" appear to hover lightly upon this "podium," each supporting a different dwelling function: eating, living, sleeping. Interior walls merely "thicken" to provide storage for the inevitable flotsam and jetsam of everyday life. The purely spatial play of interior spaces in which the architects engaged never loses sight of the house's raison d'être: to provide unimpeded views of the surrounding landscape. In this sense, its design posed a conflictual re-

lationship between space and program, between occupied space and viewing space. The two were locked in an optical-dwelling experiment as the design evolved toward a bundling of the three tubes devoted to the ocular functions of looking, seeing, and hiding. It is almost as if the optical experiments of Leonardo were lurking here as a latent reference too.

Like the huge geological outcroppings of rock that erupt into the site, what emerged from the drawing board was a trinocular "viewing machine" with a nod to the photomontage techniques that David Hockney had explored a decade earlier, and with a sequence of panoramic landscape views fanned out like a deck of cards to capture what a single image cannot. The primary view is to the south, *looking* out into the natural landscape toward the ocean; the views out the opposite side take in the first Topanga House and a sparsely developed colony of single-family residences to the north and east. But the views from any given spot inside the house are bifurcated at the tangential intersections, so that *seeing* in two directions at once is possible. And no two "framed" views from within correspond exactly: even though it is possible to see through two tubes simultaneously, what is seen is two framed views that do not converge into one; rather, they diverge, creating serial views that defy the principle of binocular vision.

With this project, the aim was to reach beyond the open plan to create *continuous space*. There is not a single door in the house. Billowing semi-sheer white curtains mounted on ceiling tracks break up the pristine white interior spaces, respecting the matter of privacy yet allowing for an element of surprise in this nearly panoptic house, since they modulate not only seeing but also what is seen, enclosing or framing spaces depending on how they are positioned. The prominent elevation of the house and its 360-degree exposure to the surrounding area—especially at night when it glows in the dark—makes *hiding* a necessity.

Coming full circle, back to Graz and the Latent Utopias installation, the question of how to clad the house was informed directly by the latex inflatable that had floated in that gallery. The problem of cladding continuous space almost automatically implied sheeting of some kind; impermeability was a priority, and resistance to fire mandatory. A stretched skin invoking the Graz inflatable was the desired effect. What emerged was a burnt-reddish, terracotta-colored, rubber-based product that seemed to fit all the technical specifications, but aesthetically was beyond the pale as far as the clients were concerned: "Red rubber with a product logo imprinted every few feet?" In the end, the logo was barely visible, and over time, the appearance of the rough-and-ready skin that so offended has receded from consciousness with a growing awareness that it will eventually be masked by the same flora that has nearly swallowed Topanga I.

What is dominant at the level of the site is the utopian project to render the Topanga Ranch an Edenic haven. As the full spectrum of functions is fine-tuned, as infrastructures are implemented, as places for animals and guests are gradually conceived, the outward appearance of everything except the nearly untouched landscape will change over time. But the house will remain both lookout post and hideaway for its occupants.

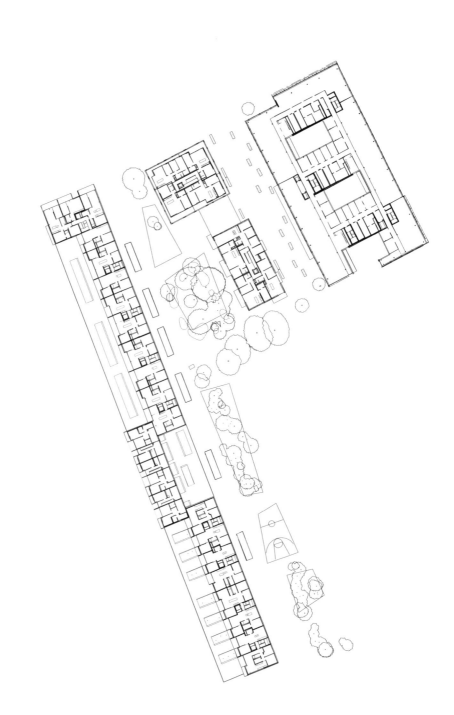

FORGING PROSPECTS

VERENA DOERFLER

Romantic. The word seems to float in space, not really at ease in contemporary architectural discourse. And yet, it belongs to this place.

Upon entering a factory workshop, one discovers an endless assortment of stone forges, anvils, pokers, and hammers in every conceivable shape and form. The interior is blackened with soot and smells of flickering fires and sweaty, backbreaking work. Only a small kitchenette equipped with a stone-aged coffee machine and all the usual kitchen utensils offers a moment of reprieve—a colorful assemblage of items thrown together some time in the 1960s. This factory building is the meeting place of the "Blacksmiths' Guild," whose members gather now and then to celebrate the past by firing up the forges and taking hammer to hand. And when it is time for a break, the blacksmiths retire to this somewhat misplaced yet wistful kitchen to brew up a pot of coffee. The place is truly anything else but modern.

At first glance, perhaps "romantic" is the perfect term to describe this scene, the industrial atmosphere tucked away in the inner courtyard of the complex, just waiting to be found—at least by those who are seeking. The workshop, a true gem of industrial culture, is at the same time the very heart of this urban development in greater Zurich where forward-looking residential and office space is currently being built. Two of the five planned residential buildings as well as an office structure have already been completed and now form an integral part of what

was once a factory site. The qualities of that site have likewise been incorporated in a new architectural and urban design concept, which despite its modern approach, and instead of simply replacing the old with the new, seeks to integrate tradition and history.

The site was witness to a bygone era—the dawning of the industrial revolution with its technical advances as well as exhausting and repetitive labor. In our digital age, work is often reduced to virtual clicks and fingers dancing across keyboards and this can often lead to feelings of nostalgia for the past. But in our yearning for the old days when "everything was better" we sometimes develop a rather warped sense of history.

Nothing was better in the past, of course. It was just different. When the old factory buildings, including the blacksmiths' workshop, were originally built in 1920, the modern age was already in full swing. Industry perfected the production of steel, the invention of the steam engine led to the steam locomotive, the advent of the railway connected the most far-flung corners, and the very first automobiles began chugging around cities. The boilers boiled, the steam engines steamed, and the workers sweated and groaned.

Ninety years separate this past from this present—or at least they do here. IntegraSquare, as the place is now called, remains an industrial premises, but one that has changed in line with the times. Today, the entire area south of the train tracks, including the land around the site, is an important development, which has set out to transform the village of Wallisellen into a city and an industrial wasteland into a new place to work and live.

The new occupants are full of praise for the industrial charm that courses through the complex. For some residents caught up in their daily routines of "virtual" work, the very fact that physical work is still being done in the adjacent factory sheds and workshops is something of an inspiration.

This may be a consequence of viewing the past through rose-tinted spectacles, but it may also be proof of the need to simply slow down, the need to "get ourselves grounded," which is a particularly difficult thing to do in a globalized and computerized world such as ours. One of the best solutions to this struggle is to combine the places in which we work, live, and play, which is precisely what the project seeks to achieve: to create a place in an industrial—and hence raw—and only rudimentarily urbanized terrain.

For in truth, they are people with a specific notion of life who choose to make their home here on the outskirts of Zurich. They cherish urbanity and see no need to separate work from their private lives. They know how important it is to have the option of withdrawing, but they still want to have a share in the creation of a new form of urban living—here on the periphery of Zurich's hustle and bustle, yet still at the very nexus of an up-and-coming urban region.

Contextualizing instead of negating the past: architecture that is embedded in and builds on what is already there—these are some of the ideas behind the project's urban concept. Without it there would be no place for the anachronism of our blacksmiths' workshop. This place of reminiscence, as a matter of fact, forms the hidden center of an architectural approach that seeks not to negate its function, but instead to integrate it as fundamental to the overall approach in which existing structures are seized upon, carried forward, and expanded. Others might have succumbed to the ease of plowing under this industrial ruin and starting from scratch.

The undertaking to transform the site was an undertaking to let urbanization take hold of Wallisellen, there where a city has never before existed. The architecture merely orders the space to contain it—nothing more and nothing less. By building on existing structures and taking them a step further, the project acknowledges that buildings can

only go so far in creating spaces that constitute urbanity. Urban development is actually more like an organic process in which architecture serves as a "stage" that must be filled with life. Which is the cue for the project. Not for nothing does the concept play on the idea of a chessboard, proceeding like chess players seeking out their next moves, so that move for move new spaces arise, where once there was only industry and empty space.

In purely architectural terms, this incremental approach is most clearly visible in the office building at Hammerweg 1, the first of several buildings to be constructed and at the same time a driving force of the whole development. This structure plays with its own geometry. The large amount of glass communicates a sense of transparency both from the inside out and vice versa. But it also melds seamlessly with its direct neighbor, an example of pragmatic modern architecture built around twenty years ago.

Just what integrated action within the context of urban development can achieve is evident here: existing buildings, even those that were perhaps not so inspired, can lend structure to the whole and—in almost game-like fashion—create something new. "It's your move," it seems to whisper.

Together, the new and existing structures stake out a boundary for the entire site. While protecting it from the noise of trains to the north, they define the public outdoor spaces at the very center of the site. The newly completed housing block functions in a similar fashion. It, too, extends from east to west along a busy street, shielding and simultaneously framing urban space. Yet whoever chooses to live here has the best of both worlds: industrial charm and seclusion.

The handling of the complex's interior space is utterly unforced. The residential buildings at Hammerweg 2 and 4, both of which are independent structures in their own right even if connected by a glass-fronted ground floor, punctuate the space and serve to break up the straightforwardness of the surrounding architecture.

Situated between these linear structures are a number of playgrounds, sport areas, and additional space for future residential buildings that combine to create a sense of openness—an openness which at the same time is the prime mover for the evolution of urbanity. But first and foremost, it is the interaction of the opposing forces of new and old which gives those who choose to live and work here the "breathing space" needed to establish a new form of living space, where work and movement existed long before the designs were even on the table. Which, in short, seeks the new in the old and vice versa.

Residents have described it in interviews as a place with "character," an "attractive" space that is "conscious of its own history," an architectural approach that is "respectful" of the past. They cherish the proximity to the village and inspiring contact with raw industrial culture. And even though it may seem something of a contradiction, the residents are spared the urban bustle that so many of Zurich's residents have to face every day.

Here in this location on the outskirts of Zurich, architecture has provided this city-like social structure with the room it needs to grow. It is an environment that interweaves the past with tomorrow's notions of living and working. And the urban pioneers who call this place their home are certainly best suited for the task. "It's your move!"

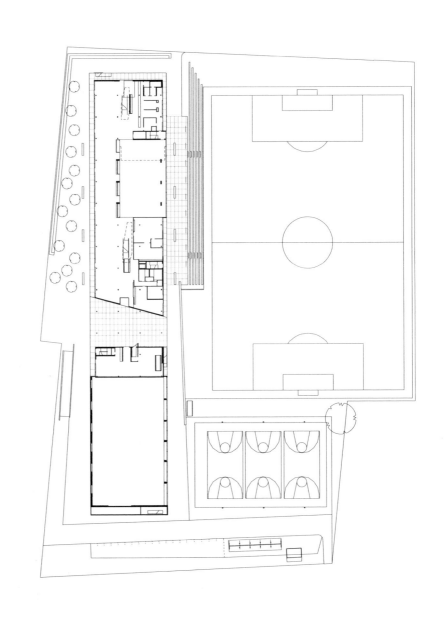

PERSEPOLIS IN ADLISWIL

CLAUDE ENDERLE

Urban architecture in Adliswil? Hard to imagine for anyone who knows the region. Flanked by the Uetliberg to the west and cut off permanently from Lake Zurich by the freeway to the east, Adliswil with its architectural relics of an idyllic rural past has all the hallmarks of a Zurich suburb. Although its current population of roughly 16,000 inhabitants and perhaps 8,000 households would theoretically make it a town, Adliswil in fact falls between two stools, being neither an autonomous village nor an administrative district of Zurich, but rather something nebulous in between.

The Adliswil region has become quite international lately, with a growing population of English-speakers from a variety of countries, and it was for these mainly upper-middle-class families that the campus of Zurich International School (ZIS) was built in southern Adliswil. Well connected to both Zug and Zurich as well as the attractive residential districts on the western shore of Lake Zurich, it is an ideal location. As a day school and meeting place for English-speaking families from abroad who spend an average of three years in Switzerland, ZIS

is well aware of architecture's social importance as something with which to identify. In an attempt to make architectural boundaries more porous and to promote integration, it has opened up the campus to private organizations, local clubs, and the municipality of Adliswil.

But does that automatically mean we must think in urban categories here? Well, if you read the project documentation written by the architects from agps who designed the building, you will find they define the institution of a school as an "ensemble of manifold connections," while referring to its material equivalent in architectural terms as an "urban organism"; so the urban comparison is imperative.

That the cities of Antiquity such as the Persian city of Persepolis can be read as multilayered, self-contained organisms, or as a whole cosmos, and may indeed have served as a prototype for modern "ensembles of manifold connections" was known long before Peter Sloterdijk's idea of spherology. When designing a school—or in this case a campus—as a place where images of the world are produced, architects have a marked tendency to draw on a broad range of possible models and antecedents.

In actual fact, though, both the image and the concept of the city changed fundamentally some time ago. Despite great efforts to reduce complexity, very little urban development these days offers an aesthetic capable of producing a world view. Urban planners would therefore be well advised to be on the lookout not so much for the kind of urban spaces that Camillo Sitte explored in his study of village and city squares in the late nineteenth century, but for deconstructivist urban "structures"—whatever that may mean.

Yet this is not the kind of image that springs to mind the first time you set eyes on the ZIS building in Adliswil. Approached from the south, it resembles neither a village-like ensemble of larger and smaller pavilions, nor indeed an artistic ensemble of various structures, each trying to communicate its function to the outsider using the symbols described by Kevin Lynch in his *Image of the City* of 1960. Having set off in search of the memorable—i.e. the easily decodable—cityscape, he identified urban structural features in paths, landmarks, edges, nodes, and districts. In other words, he evaluated urban architecture in terms of its visibility or what he called its "imageability." Is this what we will discover here?

No. What is being staged here is not a hybrid, complex feat of building with urban pretensions and an original skyline. Quite the contrary: the ZIS building is a long flat monolith stretching from west to east. The south facade is clearly divided into three floors by dark strip glazing set back behind projecting balconies that serve both as escape routes and as brises soleil. The two strips of light-colored sheet metal cladding the cornice and parapet of the top floor extend along the whole length of the facade. Running parallel to this is the parapet cladding of the second floor, which extends from the library at the far western end of the building to the cafeteria and entrance hall and from there—as part of the arch-like passageway through the building—to the gym at the eastern end.

Above the cafeteria, the silvery shimmer of the metal aprons cladding the parapets of the two upper floors is interrupted by opaque glass panels reaching as far up as the roof. This vertical caesura marks a two-story indoor garden and provides an optical counterweight to the opaque glass facade at the eastern end of the building. The grids and connectors decoratively set in the glass follow their own rhythm without seeking to concur with the concrete infrastructure of the gym shining through from within. This ornamental narrative of joints and material transitions is playfully superimposed on the minimalist main idiom of purpose-built rational architecture. The idea continues in the same vein on the north facade, where the lower floor opens out onto the soccer field. Here we find playful allusions to both industrial and office architecture. Is this an example of what architectural theorists would call the "complexity and contradiction" of urban architecture?

To call the play of elements described above a superficial phenomenon would be to do it an injustice, however, for placed prominently next to the entrance to the gym complex is the supporting structure for a staircase which—defying the architecture's own logic—is presented as a foreign body protruding from the building. The non-aligned staircases continue this theme inside the building; enclosed inside high parapets at different angles, they guide the eye upward as far as the lights on the ceiling of the top floor.

In addition to this aesthetic of vertical, horizontal, and oblique lines, architectural complexity also means structural solutions such as movable partitions allowing the flexible use of space. Spatial flexibility in this building means creating an optimal learning environment for the ZIS concept of classes of continually varying size. One of the underlying requirements for this was the positioning of the fire escapes on the facade. Relieved of this function, the corridors, which are interspersed with large empty spaces that can double as attractive plazas (so we do seem to have a reference to Camillo Sitte after all), can also be used as classroom space, as indeed they often are. Nevertheless, the inclusion of empty spaces in corridors does not necessarily imply dispensing with the traditional classroom. A number of fixed smaller units were created with particular functions in mind, such as a soundproofed room above the gym for music and rooms facing north for drawing etc. These serve as a reminder that a building also means "the organization of space in space. So is the community. So is the city," to quote Eliel Saarinen.

Now an "ensemble of manifold connections" is more than just an arrangement of things in relation to one another: it is also an arrangement of things and people. That I chose to visit the school on a

Saturday when the ground floor had been arranged to host the annual school bazaar was thus a lucky coincidence. A buzz of activity greeted me as I entered the building. In a large, light-flooded space with glass facades to the south and west, tables had been set up as sales stands where roller-skates, aerodynamic bicycles, and many other kinds of sports equipment, school materials or decorative objects for the home were being offered for sale.

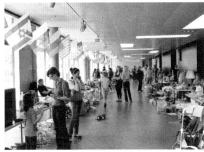

We've all been to flea markets, yet none of us would give any thought to typical school bazaar architecture—neither to its origins in the Oriental souk nor to its usually rather boring modern incarnation, also known as shopping mall. Normally school bazaars are held outside, if only because there is no suitable space inside. Not here, though. At the ZIS, the architecture seems perfectly suited to such temporary repurposing. But is repurposing really the right term? Would it not be much truer to say that limited spatial flexibility for the ephemeral or the temporary is part of the architectural concept here?

The genesis of this urban organism really ought to be conceived of in the following terms: on the right you have the freeway; on the left, somewhere in the background, the chain of hills that form the Uetliberg, Zurich's own private mountain; and to the north is Adliswil, a suburban community with a population of some 16,000 inhabitants. The view from the south, in other words, is of the village, and if you veer off the gravel path, you will find yourself on a footpath leading straight across a field. That was before the school was built. Now the axis leading to the village is more like a funnel. The passageway leading through the ground floor of the ZIS to the playing fields to the north is vaguely reminiscent of how the path used to be—and hence is one of the many layers forming the "ensemble of manifold connections" that constitutes architecture. Are there really a thousand such layers or plateaus—or is it perhaps just a question of orientation?

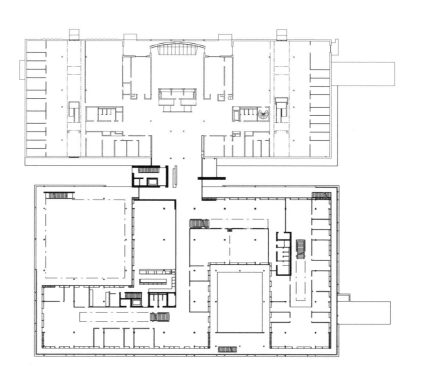

AT THE OTHER END OF THE PERISCOPE

MARGARETE VON LUPIN

Danis and Orhan pedaled at a steady pace, allowing their ingenious glider—a kind of winged bicycle—to float through the redwood plantation as if gravity had been relegated to a bygone era. The two friends were on their way back to Gland after inspecting their new production facility and before long they saw the headquarters of the International Union for Conservation of Nature looming up between four 60-foot-high black locust trees.

Danis and Orhan rolled down the ramp underneath the ground floor and all the way through into the atrium, past the rainwater catch basin and the flaky, ash-gray bark of the wild service tree (prized in the making of fine fruit brandies), and into the underground garage originally built to house automobiles.

With a combined age of around three-quarters of a century, Danis and Orhan were among the few who had maintained not only a long, but also a very personal relationship with the building. It was almost as if their lives would have taken a completely different course had this conservation center in Gland never been built.

They climbed the stairs up to the second, much larger atrium on the ground floor: a spacious terrace which Danis and Orhan liked to call their "Think Station." There on this warm February afternoon they greeted two of their colleagues, who along with their two guests were grabbing themselves a cup of coffee in the adjacent bar, now known as the "Think Pump." The terrace with its patinated tropical woods, which for over forty years had stood up to all sorts of wind and weather and had lent the place its unyielding character, was extremely popular.

Danis and Orhan had rented two offices in the IUCN extension nearly forty years after it was first built. Since then, it had become a thriving world-class center of environmental technology, and Gland had changed beyond recognition. It had freed itself from the monotonous urban agglomeration extending from Lausanne to Geneva and was now blossoming in precisely that unplanned fashion that is typical of booming megacities.

Danis, an environmental engineer, and Orhan, a producer of climate envelopes, had chosen to locate their own flourishing business in Gland as well. After earning degrees in their respective fields of study, the pair had gained sufficient work experience by participating in a variety of experiments and projects. They had then decided to team up and together with their research group had succeeded in developing a type of textile fiber capable of maintaining a balance between perspiration, heat, and cold. The breathable fabric was able to maintain a constant body temperature—keeping you warm when it is cold and cool when it is hot. Mass production of the material had led to its worldwide proliferation, which in turn had resulted in a long-overdue revaluation of the role of clothing as both a covering for the body and as a bearer of multiple functions—to say nothing of the latest fashions with which innumerable designers and labels sought to cater to all tastes and budgets.

The invention had made the heating and cooling of buildings redundant, especially as the climate of Central Europe had begun to resemble that of the Mediterranean and subtropical zones. "And … is everything still on track?" Their coworkers naturally wanted to know what they were up to.

"Yes, I think we'll have to get started," replied Orhan, nodding in a demonstration of his eagerness to get going laid on for his colleagues' benefit; whereupon he and Danis disappeared into the entrance area. Orhan wanted to stop by the reception desk.

"Have you already submitted the textile pattern?" Orhan asked, exuding his customary charm—a charm that was at its most beguiling when it was up to him to ensure that the first models in a new collection were sufficiently flattering of their young customers lithe forms. Then one or two IUCN employees dropped by and their quick exchange of words soon led to a longer, more animated discussion.

At this point, Danis leaned back against the elegant gray wall of insulating concrete. Their choice of this material for the expansion—a benchmark in environmental building techniques—had won IUCN international praise as an environmentally-aware building client. Danis liked to stand here, for the cavernous reception area had become a natural meeting point for all those who played a role in protecting the earth's environment: small groups of experts engrossed in conversation hurrying back and forth between the old and new buildings with their old-fashioned electronic reading and communication devices; purposeful sales representatives; guests who came to eat and relax at the Think Station; school groups on their way to the visitors' center on the second floor; delegates from all over the world who instead of looking for the "Red List" training room followed the signs down here to one of the two exhibition rooms on the ground floor; television crews for live broadcasts; activists and government representatives.

Leaning against this wall, as he had so often done before, and following the mounting bustle in the reception area from an amused distance, Orhan's thoughts drifted back to the earliest days in the building's history.

As young teenagers from Zurich's fourth district, Denis and Orhan regularly went down to the old freight yard for soccer practice. One day on their way to practice, they heard two voices engaged in a heated discussion quite near to where they were standing. They followed the voices until they found themselves at the open window of an architects' studio, where they stopped to eavesdrop on the passionate debate in progress inside.

They listened to the architects wracking their brains in an effort to figure out how to design a new building—the building in which Danis was now standing—in compliance with the strictest environmental building codes of the day, the LEED Platinum and the Minergie-P-Eco. Danis had never understood why the LEED Platinum certification had been named after a precious metal whose mining in South Africa for use in catalytic converters in the northern hemisphere had caused so much social and environmental damage. In retrospect he realized that although serious and dedicated, when viewed in their entirety the various steps taken to move away from fossil fuels and towards renewable and carbon-free means of energy production had been completely uncoordinated and unsystematic. Humans were capable of solving individual problems, but they seldom considered the consequences and side-effects of their actions. The very fact that solar energy production had spawned another menace, namely "electricity usage with a clean conscience," for example, was something people had chosen to ignore from the outset. The technologies continued to advance, but the core problem remained.

The insulating concrete that so often set Danis's thoughts in motion, however, had remained a sought-after building material—particularly after it was developed into a form of carbon-free recycled insulating concrete which had made the absurd complexity of building envelopes redundant virtually overnight. The use of multilayered forms of building insulation had been considered a sustainable solution only in the earliest days of the carbon-free hype.

"Let's get started." Orhan always got a kick out of rubbing his sleeve against his friend's—he liked the quiet crinkly sound that it made. They walked up the new central staircase past the wall painted with silver pigment and entered the large passageway connecting the old and new buildings. IUCN insiders called it "The Bridge" since they liked to imagine how here at the helm they could steer the ship of government and use the pressure of public opinion to set the course in favor of ecological systems and environmental protection.

It was here that Danis and Orhan ran into their two project partners: Tuula and Yuri were just coming down the stairs and beginning to look relaxed after a session in the "Think Tank." Together with a few captain- and hero-category project managers, they had just finished one of their legendary, relentlessly sobering rituals—a subject of both fear and awe—aimed at neutralizing any form of mental garbage. It was up there in the periscope-turned-architecture that reached up into the skies and left all the confusion down below that they came together to switch on their brains, to dine in style, to celebrate generous gestures, to gain momentum for great thinking, and to look into the future. It was up there that they were able to elegantly accomplish all that usually got lost in the fog of complexity and relentless bean counting that reduced even the best of thinkers to small-mindedness.

Together Danis, Orhan, Tuula, and Yuri made their way through the new building towards their shared office which they had redesigned specially for this new endeavor. They greeted each other like friends and tried to ignore the fact that the top floor again looked as if it were so full of people that it could burst at any second.

Visitors were standing in line hoping to get a seat for the live broadcast in the Red List training center. Ever since the room had been trans-

formed into a television studio, there had been a run on the limited number of seats. IUCN had decided it was time reach out to a much larg-er audience with its weekly broadcasts. In the meantime, audiences had started to show as much interest in the race to prevent the extinction of endangered plants and animals as had previously been expended on events like the soccer world championships. Everyone hoped that at least the migratory birds would make it.

Danis, Orhan, Tuula, and Yuri squeezed their way through The Bridge to the offices on the other side. They walked past coworkers in conference seated at long black tables. The courses held in the small and large conference rooms had been a great hit for over two decades. Here, real-estate speculators were reschooled for participation in the govern-ment-mandated program to promote the cultivation of tropical-like timber throughout Europe.

There was very little in this building that did not have some spe-cial significance for Danis and Orhan. This long black table, for exam-ple, had been set up at their own request, as had two others in the two-story, top-lit middle zones. There had simply been no suitable places where they could hold their numerous spontaneous conferences—or even those meetings that were bound to prove controversial. The mid-dle zones, however, turned out to be a true blessing, an architectural luxury. This was thanks largely to the arcades stretching along the length of the entire building, which because they doubled as the escape routes required by fire protection laws meant that the internal fire load was no longer an issue. Now, at last, there was an official place for even the most heated and unrelenting disputes between opposing interests.

Once in their office, Danis, Orhan, Tuula, and Yuri got straight down to business. There was very little time and what was needed most was a sharp intellect and analytical exactitude. Tuula was an architect who had made a name for herself with her historical investigations into the topic of low-tech versus high-tech architectural strategies. Yuri, a building recycling specialist, brought with him a great deal of technical know-how, which he combined with an expert understanding of economics and management.

The four had been tasked with simplifying the IUCN building's technical systems in line with the new utilities management regulations. New, climate-adaptive cladding had been added so that the building stayed warm in winter. Heating and cooling systems were thus no longer necessary. New energy usage regulations meant that electricity consumption had had to be significantly reduced, while the metals reclamation agreement required the comprehensive dismantling of all above-ground metals such as copper.

All this had become necessary because earlier resolutions and promises aimed at reducing consumption had turned out to be nothing more that empty words, mere lip service, wheeling and dealing. The West had run out of raw materials and the mining rights to Afghanistan's immense mineral resources had been snapped up by China in return for hastily constructed, practical, and inexpensive housing, schools, hospitals, and streets at the start of the last Afghan War. Afghan women and girls, whom the West had attempted to win over with democracy and education, now spoke Chinese as a second language.

Danis, Orhan, Tuula, and Yuri had rented neighboring private offices. Each of the 120-square-feet offices—the standard office size in the old building—had a door and a ceiling-to-floor window leading out into the arcade. During the summer the windows were shaded by bottom-to-top sun screens, while in winter the sun heated the building through the glass. As the supporting structure allowed the interior walls to be removed, the four of them had been able to create a large, light-flooded office for their shared activities.

"I hate to admit it, but it really pained me when we had to remove the clever climate-control system"—Yuri was always wracked by melancholic bouts of nostalgia whenever they were forced to dismantle any of the building's magnificent technical systems. They knew from closer inspection that not only had the previous heating and cooling system been extremely sophisticated, at least for a system installed at a time when no one really knew what the word "energy" actually meant—"but the architects built this building like a slumbering machine that would awaken only when it was truly needed."

Orhan could see in Danis's eyes where his thoughts were at that moment. Tuula took the opportunity to lay down one of her usual canny synopses. "All that is left of it for future generations is an entertaining riddle: As soon as someone enters the room, a CO_2 sensor on the ceiling panel activates a ventilator in a climate-control box on the floor. Fresh air from outside flows into the box past pipes filled with a fluid like water or glycol. The pipes in the form of a heat pump are attached to underground geothermal probes. This allows us to use the earth, with its average temperature of 12 degrees centigrade, as a huge reservoir of stored heat. Depending on the season, the fluid in the pipes is warmed or cooled—supported by a heat pump when necessary. The warmed or cooled fresh air flows through the climate box and into the room. The exhausted air is removed through the ventilation ducts installed in the ceiling panels above the middle zones. And the system functions independently in every room, making it a decentralized system."

Danis and Orhan did not find this at all amusing. They had been reluctant to take on the project from the start. For them it was as if the passionate debate they had overheard as young teenagers standing outside a window had taken place just yesterday. They still could not believe just how much the architects had staked on this new and untried climate control system. Who else until then had taken seriously the Brundtland Report with its calls for intergenerational environmental justice and sustainable development, according to which the needs of the present could be met only as long as the needs of future generations were not put at risk?

Slowly the skies darkened; they had had the shortest day of the year just a short while ago. The artificial lighting system consisting of LED lamps had switched itself on in the twilight. Danis, Orhan, Tuula, and Yuri would soon have to present a concept describing how the dismantling of the building could be accompanied by a tectonically based fresh air supply for all rooms. Their heated debate and sharp exchange of words could be heard long into the night.

After saying goodbye, Danis and Orhan made their way through the arcade to the external staircase. The lights had already gone off in most of the offices, and as they passed by the windows they could no longer see inside all the human-inhabited—almost eccentric—biotopes the way they could during the day.

Danis and Orhan again found a seat at their Think Station. The Think Pump had just filled their glasses with a refreshingly cold Bière Glandestine. They settled back in the armchairs and delighted in their first sips of beer.

Orhan looked along the side of the building up toward the star-spattered sky. "Remember how we used to conduct our meetings up there in the Think Tank, and how that connecting box between the two buildings with its captivating panorama of Lake Geneva and the Alps proved to be the best place for us to get our funding together?" Danis and Orhan clinked glasses.

"Yes," answered Danis. "When I think back on how the shed-like photovoltaic system basically defined the building's outward design, its jagged crown… Does anyone now remember how the design of the facade parapets came about? Or how solar energy was generated in those days?"

Danis and Orhan slowly lapsed into silence. In fact, the whole world lay at their feet on this pleasantly warm and peaceful February evening, so there was no need for all of this inner turmoil. But it was as if the world had once again ceased to be the place they had come to expect, as if by turning slowly on its course, it had imperceptibly left the two friends behind without their noticing, removing them from the very place where they had wanted to discuss their next course of action. Danis and Orhan thus lived their lives as they always had: happily ever after, but vigilant.

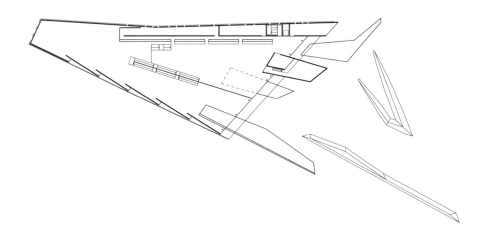

LESS IS
THE FUTURE

The Children's Museum of Los Angeles was founded about thirty years ago in a provisional space downtown. After "temporarily" closing its doors on August 27, 2000, to focus on an expanded public-private initiative spanning the greater metropolitan area, the museum's Board of Governors unveiled a project to develop two ambitious "campuses." Identified as one of these was a plateau overlooking Hansen Dam in Lake View Terrace at the far north end of the San Fernando Valley; the parcel was leased to the museum by the City of Los Angeles in 2000 for fifty years. The other projected site was in Little Tokyo. Despite the fact that the Hansen Dam and Little Tokyo campuses were both launched on what could be described as shaky financial ground, there was talk early on of additional sites being developed "in due course." As the process unfolded and a series of roadblocks emerged, one after the other the playing fields were leveled to a single campus—and even that proved difficult to realize.

Having projected museums for other cities in competitions for the Arizona Natural History Museum in Mesa, the Nam June Paik Museum in Seoul, and the Mercedes Benz Museum in Stuttgart, the architects grasped the task in all its many facets. In 2000, a jury of critics and deans of architecture schools in collaboration with the Board of Governors of the Children's Museum selected Thom Mayne of Morphosis for Little Tokyo, and agps to design the Hansen Dam campus. Three key ideas characterized the agps project: that the building itself would be didactic, becoming an "exhibit" in its own right, displaying its structure, materials, and renewable energy systems, as well as arousing curiosity; that the spaces and circulation systems would belong to dynamic sequences and itineraries, with paths leading into and through the open and flexible gallery spaces on two levels, as well as out onto the planted rooftop and into the surrounding parkland; and that the museum would be integrated into the infrastructural landscape of the Hansen Dam Recreational Park. Plantings on the building's roof were projected to offset solar gain, while geothermal air cooling was to be augmented with water misters, and solar energy deployed to cool as well as power the whole building.

The architects were commissioned in early 2001. Alex Padilla, councilman for the San Fernando Valley district which includes Hansen Dam, fortuitously became president of the Los Angeles City Council that same year. Padilla was able to forge professional and financial partnerships at all levels to fuel the project for the "Valley's first public museum." Then came the cataclysmic events of September 11, 2001, creating, among other things, an economic climate in which it was im-

possible to sustain the museum's laudable mission. Funding proved increasingly elusive, but the project still moved forward, and in 2002, the *Next LA Award* of the American Institute of Architects (AIA) went to agps for its Children's Museum. Impressed by the project for Hansen Dam, the jury drew special attention to the fact that "the architects have inventively rewritten the program to include the building's external and internal systems as a featured exhibit in this energy-conscious children's museum."

Ironically, by 2002 the choice of the Hansen Dam site had become cause for suspicion in some quarters. Many felt it had been calculated to turn the tide of public opinion on the Valley's bid to secede from the City of Los Angeles. Residents at the northern end of the Valley took the stance that they had long been deprived of equitable city services and amenities, and Hansen Dam, one of California's five "flood control basins," was implicated in this. The dam was constructed in the 1940s, though the reservoir behind it was allowed to fill up with water only after World War II. A "sand beach" was created to form the "shore" of the "lake," but as silt from the Tujunga Wash built up over time, the "lake" filled in. In a feeble attempt to tame nature, a pool and make-believe "beach" were installed.

Still, despite being engulfed by a gloomy social, political, and economic climate, the Children's Museum at Hansen Dam went all the way through to the final phase, meaning that the technical drawings were two-thirds complete by the time it was put on hold in 2004 on the grounds that the funding deficit was "insurmountable."

A year later, in 2005, a new proposition was on the table. The director of the Children's Museum approached agps again to ask if they could produce the building for half the original budget; or could they produce something in the order of a big-box store instead? The former was not feasible, the latter not palatable, but the wheels began to turn, and the architects were invited to redesign the museum. The idea of a simpler project, of scaling back the size of the building and certain elements of the program, of turning to industrial concrete fabrication methods, and of streamlining aesthetic elements seemed plausible, even desirable—especially since the Hansen Dam campus was intended to model environ-

mental sustainability. The underlying principle in the second design phase became "less is the future." As the architects put it, the building would be "tougher (and rougher) in its architectural expression," but they were nevertheless intent on ensuring that radical cost-cutting did not deteriorate into false economies. A sustainable balance was apparently struck: like the first project, the redesign submitted by agps received a 2005 Merit Award from the AIA.

As built, the museum emerges from the ground at its western end, where Foothill Boulevard and Osborne Street frame the narrow, low-slung streetfront. Here the building height is that of a small child—just four feet. A sunken basin on this side harvests the rain water cascading over the roof, providing an efficient form of storm water management. On the eastern side, a garden opens out toward the park and the dam, expanding to fill its trapezoidal site. From the front end or "nose" of the museum, the building rises to a height of 36 feet at the entrance, and follows the slope of the site. Economic tilt-up concrete was used to enclose the building envelope, its thermal mass shielding the interior from solar heat gain. This effect was to be reinforced by a photovoltaic membrane applied in a "cow-spot" pattern to make a display of energy conservation. Three small pavilions (housing a bookstore, ticket office, and theater) line a path leading from the park to the museum entrance, where its great canopy captures prevailing winds for ventilation. The mechanical systems collected together in a single structure will gradually be overgrown with plantings, and a children's vegetable garden is projected for the space in between.

The museum's structural members are visible on the interior, and the energy and climate control systems are likewise made legible. Interior finishing is being projected in phases, as funds become available. The exhibition galleries on two levels have been conceived as open and flexible enough to accommodate an infinite variety and number of programs, while in the center of the double-height ground-floor space, a children's reading circle is laid out. Nearby, a bright crimson bridge-like ramp leads up to the second gallery floor. Throughout, colored light effects and novel materials instill utilitarian spaces and interior fittings with a sense of *play*, just as the calculated scaling of amenities like

drinking fountains (installed at three different heights to accommodate growing children of all ages) adds a humorous edge.

An enlightened project involving advanced ecological thinking, the Children's Museum was fraught with difficulties at the institutional level. The Board of Governors proved to be unstable and increasingly disengaged from the construction process. Although the architects were graced with a contractor who could balance the cost-craft equation and felt a genuine commitment to quality results, the project managers and museum directors who oversaw the process continually shifted. Fast-forward to April 2009: The building was nearly complete, if still plagued by funding shortfalls, when another set of extraordinary and unforeseeable circumstances forced the museum's Board of Governors (which by now included California Senator Alex Padilla) to relinquish their tenuous hold on both the building and the site, leaving the fate of the 57,000-square-foot structure uncertain. One of the museum's largest donors was indicted for fraud, and as he had already transferred approximately a quarter of his ill-gained wealth to the board, the Children's Museum was under obligation to return it as money tainted by scandal.

It is impossible to tell the story of the Children's Museum without acknowledging its problematic history, or what the architects call its "odyssey." To be sure, their conviction that "impossible-to-predict transformations" are part of the life of a building has been tested by fire, and the Children's Museum designed by agps may yet become something else without ever having functioned as a museum. In the absence of a so-called "angel" donor of the kind who sweeps in at the last minute with a benevolent gift, many believe that there will never be a museum for children in Los Angeles. Never is a long time, but the building has effectively been taken over by the City of Los Angeles (which paid the lion's share of the construction costs), and to date, city officials have said publicly only that they "hope it will continue to be used for an education function." With the core and shell of the museum completed, one remaining question is whether the building is flexible and durable enough to survive the financial storm in which it is embroiled, or to find a new purpose. Another is whether it is possible for *architectural space* generated for a particular cultural purpose to become a generator of *social space*, despite a radical change of purpose. And then there is the question of limits: Where will the constant reduction of resources from "less to less to less" lead? As one of the architects remarked, ultimately "the future has been taken away." A completely different set of questions is that pertaining to the sustainability of cultural institutions in a world in which less is indeed destined to be the standard for the foreseeable future.

B2 FRIDAY, APRIL 3, 2009   Los Angeles Times

UNCERTAIN FUTURE: The 97,000-square-foot Children's Museum of Los Angeles in the Hansen Dam Recreation Area is unlikely to open because of questions surrounding a $10-million donation from a man accused of investment fraud.

Fraud case hurts museum

SEC allegations against a donor who pledged $10 million may force Children's Museum of L.A. into bankruptcy.

BY STUART PFEIFER

Investment fraud allegations against a Sherman Oaks businessman may have been a fatal blow to a struggling San Fernando Valley children's museum to which Bruce F. Friedman pledged $10 million last year.

Absent an unexpected "angel" donation, the Children's Museum of Los Angeles plans to file for liquidation under Chapter 7 of federal bankruptcy laws and cease operations, director Cecilia Aguilera Glassman said Thursday.

Construction of a 97,000-square-foot building for the museum in the Hansen Dam Recreation Area was completed in 2007. But the facility has sat empty since then because museum officials were not able to raise the funds needed to buy exhibits and cover operating costs.

Some devastating news came last month, when the Securities and Exchange Commission filed a lawsuit accusing Friedman of diverting more than $17 million from investors in his Sherman Oaks company, Diversified Lending Group, and persuaded a judge to freeze all the company's assets.

Friedman's charity, the Friedman Charitable Foundation, pledged $10 million to the children's museum in 2007, making it the museum's largest donor. But the museum received "less than half" of the pledge and has not determined whether it can keep the money, Glassman said.

Without the $10-million gift, the museum would be about $22 million short of the $58.5 million it needs to open, Glassman said.

The museum's board of governors, which includes state Sen. Alex Padilla (D-Pacoima) and former Assemblymen Mike Ross and Richard Katz, voted March 27 to declare bankruptcy.

Museum officials have been in discussions with a court-appointed receiver managing Friedman's assets to determine whether the museum needs to return the money it has received from Friedman. Meanwhile, the FBI and U.S. attorney's office have opened a criminal investigation into Friedman's operations.

The museum had not received a single donation since the SEC's action against Friedman was disclosed. It had about $100,000 in the last month when concerned donors rescinded their pledges, Glassman said.

"The only thing that could change the course is if there were one or more angel donors who would step in and see the value of the project," Glassman said. "Otherwise, we'll probably not see a children's museum in Los Angeles."

The children's museum operated for about 30 years downtown before closing in 2000 amid plans for the San Fernando Valley facility.

The city of Los Angeles, which paid for much of the building's construction costs, may end up owning the modern, angular building, said City Councilman Richard Alarcon.

"Some of the ideas are a charter school or some kind of educational program. We'll be reaching out to some folks to see if that's a possibility," Alarcon said.

The SEC, in its lawsuit against Friedman, contended he diverted millions from investors to his charity and himself, spending the stolen money on luxuries that included a $4.5-million Malibu home, expensive cars, designer jewelry and clothing.

In addition to its donation to the museum, the Friedman foundation had pledged $5 million to the Dodgers Dream Foundation to help build youth baseball fields throughout Southern California.

Dodgers officials said Friedman never paid any of the money and is no longer part of the project.

stuart.pfeifer@latimes.com

PROJECT INFORMATION

Hollywood House, Los Angeles
→ **Page 11**
1991–1993; *Client* Marc Angélil and Sarah Graham, Los Angeles; *Consultants* Ove Arup & Partners California, structural engineering; Kelly Hames, Grendel Construction Inc., general contractor; John McCoy, Steel Art, steel fabricator

Trüb House, Horgen
→ **Page 29**
1996–1998; *Client* Patrick und Karin Trüb, Horgen; *Consultants* APT Ingenieure GmbH, structural engineering; Blumer Elementtechnik AG, wood construction, computer integrated manufacturing; Trüb AG Gartenbau, landscape design

Office Building, Train Station Winterthur
→ **Page 43**
2002–2010; *Competition* 2001; *Client* Swiss Federal Railways (SBB), Bern; *Associates* GMS Partner AG, construction management; Blanca Blarer, artist (conceptual design and canopy); *Consultants* APT Ingenieure GmbH, structural engineering; Amstein + Walthert AG, mechanical engineering and energy concept; Stäger & Nägeli AG, facade engineering; Braun Brandsicherheit AG, fire safety consultant

Adaptive Reuse of a Laundry Factory, Zurich
→ **Page 61**
1998–2000; *Competition* 1997; *Client* Lienhardt & Partner Privatbank AG, Zurich; *Associates* Blanca Blarer, artist (color concept and *garde-corps* railing); *Consultants* APT Ingenieure GmbH, structural engineering; Getec Zürich AG, mechanical engineering and energy concept; ARGE Ganz / Kuhn Truninger, landscape design

Flickflauder Restaurant at Hof Weissbad, Appenzell
→ **Page 79**
2003–2004; *Competition* 2003; *Client* KW Kurhotel Weissbad AG, Appenzell; *Consultants* Blumer-Lehmann AG, wood construction, computer integrated manufacturing; APT Ingenieure GmbH, structural engineering; Thieme-Klima AG, mechanical systems; Hersche Ingenieure AG, environmental systems

Lunch Shelters, Los Angeles Unified School District
→ **Page 93**
1990–1992; *Client* Los Angeles Unified School District, Los Angeles; *Consultants* Ove Arup & Partners California, structural engineering; ARL & Associates, mechanical engineering; John McCoy, Steel Art, steel fabricator

Koreatown Storefronts, Los Angeles
→ **Page 103**
1992; *Client* Fixel Realty, Los Angeles; *Consultants* William Koh, structural engineering; John McCoy, Steel Art, steel fabricator

agps

Marc Angélil studied architecture at the ETH Zurich, where he also completed his doctorate. He taught at the Graduate School of Design at Harvard University and subsequently at the University of Southern California in Los Angeles. He is currently professor in the Department of Architecture at the ETH Zurich. He is the author of several books, including *Deviations—A Manual* on methods of teaching, *Indizien* on the political economy of contemporary urban territories, and *Cities of Change—Addis Ababa*.

Sarah Graham holds a Bachelor of Arts in Art History and Design from Stanford University and a Master of Architecture from Harvard University. She has been adjunct professor at the University of Southern California in Los Angeles and visiting professor at Rhode Island School of Design, Harvard Graduate School of Design, the University of California Berkeley, and Nanjing University. Sarah Graham is a fellow of the Bund Schweizer Architekten (BSA) and the American Institute of Architects (AIA).

Manuel Scholl graduated from the ETH Zurich in 1988. After acquiring several years of experience in firms of architects in southern Switzerland and Spain, he returned to Zurich, becoming an active partner of agps in 1993. Additionally, he has served as a juror for various competitions and is a board member of the Ernst Schindler Foundation for travel grants. He has been a fellow of the Bund Schweizer Architekten (BSA) since 2001. He has been involved in teaching and research at the ETH Zurich and has been professor of urban design at the Leibniz University of Hanover since 2009.

Reto Pfenninger studied architecture at the School of Engineering in Winterthur and the Academy of Fine Arts in Munich. He joined the Zurich section of the BSA in 2001 and from 2001 to 2006 was a member of the "Stadtbildkommission" in Zug. He has been a professor at the University of Applied Sciences in Northwestern Switzerland since 2006 and professor of design and construction since 2010. His main research area addresses housing development in large agglomerations.

Hanspeter Oester studied architecture at the ETH Zurich and founded his own practice in his hometown in 1995. After working for various firms of architects active both in Switzerland and abroad, including SAM in Zurich, he joined agps as a partner in 2004. He is an active member of the Schweizerische Ingenieur- und Architektenverein (SIA) in Zurich. His work focuses on the subject of sustainable development in building construction and its potential for architecture.

mark adams, corinne aebischer, marnie amato, balz amrein, marc angélil, dominik arioli, daniel arnold, joe baldwin, garo balmanoukian, diele bath, karin baumann, jeanette beck, claudine berger, harriet bersier, ivo bertolo, tobias biegger, alexander bierer, monika blach, stephan bohne, philipp bollier, ida braendstrup-richter, britta brauer, john brockway, corinne brugger, philipp brunnschweiler, michael bühler, chet callahan, maria del pilar canamero, danny cao, ursina caprez, eduardo cardozo, gisella chacòn jo, hommy chan, anastasia congdon, desirée cuttat, patrick dachtler, simon de jong, franca de jonge, matthias denzler, denise diaz de leon castelazo, alysa dunning, russel dykann, stephan eggimann, oliver eiholzer, mark ericson, keith evans, markus fahner, lukas felder, simon filler, sandra flury, thomas fotheringham, david freeland, nicholas frei, mark frey, bruce fullerton, maike funk, marcin ganczarski, alexander gaudlitz, raffael gaus, markus gontarz, michael gräfensteiner, sarah graham, thurman grant, luis grilo, hans gritsch, michael gruber, michael häge, sally harris, vera hartmann, gabi hauser, philippe hauzinger, heikki heer, mic hendriksen, dagmar heppner, thomas hildebrand, michael hirschbichler, andreas hochstrasser, rémy hofer, alyssa holmquist, sebastian hurni, sancho igual, jan henning ipach, peter jenni, rolf jenni, sharon johnston, gant jones, gopal joshi, john kaisner, severin keller, wolfgang kessler, jan kiefer, tobias klauser, bettina klinge, this kobelt, jochen köhler, samuel konrad, andreas kopp, thomas kovari, nele kräher, rüdiger kreiselmayer, jesse lecavalier, mark lee, johannes leibundgut, petra lenschow, michele lenzi, gérard lerner, christian liechti, roman loretan, moshik mah, dashne mahmoud, frank maldonado, ilinca manaila, wendy marno, marta marszal, marcel mathis, illaria mazzoleni, samuel meier, christian meili, sabine merz, gaudenz metzger, patric micheli, philipp mohr, monika moor, mark motonaga, kristina mueller, brigitte münger, simone munkel, benjamin muschg, roger naegeli, juho nyberg, hanspeter oester, manuel oswald, caroline pachoud, william paluch, tony paradowski, dario papalo, sandro peier, reto pfenninger, michael pfister, anthony poon, riley pratt, katja rapold, yves reinacher, nicole renz, georg rinderknecht, daniel roos, philipp röösli, julia rubin, silvia rüfenacht, nicolas rüst, lukas sailer, cynthia salah, benjamin sander, philipp schaefle, barbara schaub, angelika scherer, simone schmaus, nicole schneider, lukas schnider, manuel scholl, moritz schöndorf, henrike schrade, katia schröder, barbara schwab, thomas schwendener, lara semler, erik seyffarth, philipp sigg, peter sigrist, ryan smith, roman sokalski, ines specker, dennis spinnler, phil steffen, susan stevens, thomas summermatter, alexandra tanner, simon tholen, raffael thut, kai timmermann, christoph tobler, rico traxler, ines trenner, patrik uihlein, denise ulrich, scott utterstrom, christian verasani, christoph vetter, frano violich, barbara vogel, thoya vogel, christoph von ah, sabine von fischer, caroline von monschaw, patrick von planta, patrick walther, pascale wappel, greg wartak, viviane weber, andreas weiz, torsten wieders, james woolum, walter zausch, daniele zeo, martin zimmerli, daniela ziswiler

AUTHORS

Denise Bratton is an art, architectural, and urban historian and editor based in Los Angeles. She collaborated with the founding director of the Getty Center for the History of Art and the Humanities on various publications and research projects (1986–1993), and has been a consultant for the Canadian Centre for Architecture since 2002. Her publications include English translations of André Corboz, Françoise Choay, Gilles Clément, and Phyllis Lambert.

Verena Doerfler studied cultural sciences in Berlin/Potsdam. She has worked on a range of cultural projects and has curated exhibitions, including installations for the Berlin Biennale for Contemporary Art and KW Institute. In 2007, she joined the editorial staff of *DU* and *archithese*, where she worked as an editor until 2009. As a freelance journalist, she is currently working on the exhibition "100 Years Max Frisch" for the Literaturmuseum Strauhof in Zurich.

Claude Enderle lectures in theory at the Department of Interior Design and Scenography at Basel School of Design. After training as an interior and product designer at the FFI Basel and gaining extensive experience in this field, he studied history of art, economic and social history, and philosophy at the University of Zurich, completing his doctorate there in 2005. He is now a research associate in the Department of Architecture at the ETH Zurich, where he also held the post of Jasmin Grego guest lecturer from 2006 to 2008. He is the author of several publications on architecture and design.

Andrea Helbling is an architectural photographer based in Zurich. After studying photography at the Zurich School of Design, she began her career in the studio of Heinrich Helfenstein before founding her own agency Arazebra in 1995. Having at first alternated between the role of photographer and that of film lighting technician, she now works mainly as the former, producing photographs for firms of architects, magazines, and public agencies. The focus of her own photographic projects and exhibitions is on urban space in the context of everyday situations.

Margarete von Lupin is a journalist and author of numerous essays on architecture. Her research addresses the role of dialogue as a method in design, architecture, and urban studies at the interface with ethnology. She taught at the Academy for Media and Design at Ravensburg/Weingarten University of Applied Sciences and at Zurich University of the Arts (ZHdK). She is currently a lecturer in urban identity, design theory, and qualitative research at the ZHdK.

Benjamin Muschg is an architect, architectural critic, and journalist. After studying in the Department of Architecture at the ETH Zurich, he worked as a designer for various firms of architects in Zurich and during that time became increasingly engaged in discourse on architectural criticism. As a freelance journalist, he has published several essays for architecture and art magazines. He is currently a sports reporter for the Swiss newspaper *Tages-Anzeiger* and the author of a regular column on ice hockey.

ACKNOWLEDGEMENTS

The assemblage of people that contributed to this publication is as multifaceted as the book itself. The team of agps would like to express its gratitude to all the many individuals who participated in this endeavor.

Tremendously valuable to us were our discussions with the authors, who in addition to viewing the works themselves from some unexpected angles supported our undertaking with their insightful comments: Denise Bratton, Verena Doerfler, Margarete von Lupin, Claude Enderle, and Benjamin Muschg.

The photographic work of Andrea Helbling that sought to view the architecture from an everyday perspective constitutes a project in its own right. Her incidental photographs explore latent traits of use that are just as much a part of the buildings as their architectural manifestation.

Jürg Schönenberger's extraordinary work in developing and realizing the graphic concept shaped the book and sharpened its content.

Special thanks go to Thomas Kramer and his team at Scheidegger & Spiess Publishers in Zurich as well as to the translators and editors for putting the finishing touches on the publication.

We are also deeply indebted to Pascale Wappel and Dominique Leutwyler for their patient endurance and unsurpassed dedication in holding the group together.

Last but not least, the production of buildings relies fundamentally on complex collaborations. These are at the core of this book. We would therefore like to extend our sincerest thanks to all those who have contributed to the making of our buildings.

The artist Blanca Blarer, a virtual accomplice who has produced a series of art works in partnership with agps, has been working on a parallel book which is being released concurrently with this publication.

Additional photographers

Michael Arden: pp. 16, 190

Ralph Bensberg: pp. 34, 116, 119

Alain Bucher: pp. 235, 238, 242

Eduard Hueber: pp. 96, 98, 99, 100, 101, 150, 152

Eric Staudenmaier: pp. 138, 139, 142, 143, 192, 196/197, 256

Gaston Wicky: p. 166

Reinhard Zimmermann: pp. 32, 44, 46, 48, 50, 69, 82, 84, 167, 179, 180, 206, 207, 208, 209

Picture credits

p. 12: *Safety Last*, Film by Fred C. Newmeyer and Sam Taylor 1923

p. 13: David Wallace, *Hollywoodland*, 2002 (Photography 1924)

p. 17: *Arts and Architecture*, Cover designed by Ray Eames, April 1943

p. 18: *The Architectural Review*, Cover by Julius Shulman, June 1994

p. 30: Drawing Lino Trüb

p. 52: Winterthur Stadtbibliothek, INSA Gesellschaft für Schweizerische Kunstgeschichte, p. 15,

p. 83: Goldzack rubber-band factory, Gossau, *Das Erlebnis Ingenieur zu sein*, Birkhäuser, p. 22

p. 115: Peter Fischli and David Weiss, *Airport.* 1989, © Fischli/Weiss

p. 132: *Portland Monthly*, October 2007, Fall Fashion Special, Photographies Rafael Astorga

p. 194: David Hockney, sketchbook Brooklyn, November 1987, © David Hockney

p. 235: © Holcim Foundation for Sustainable Construction, Photography Alain Bucher

p. 238: © Holcim Foundation for Sustainable Construction, Photography Alain Bucher

p. 242: © Holcim Foundation for Sustainable Construction, Photography Alain Bucher

p. 259: *Los Angeles Times*, April 3, 2009

Literature

p. 65: Marcel Meili, "Die Zeiten verschleifen," in *archithese*, special issue Sarnafil Plattform, Sulgen/Zurich 2001.

p. 115: Felix E. Müller, "Modern und rentabel, ja nicht auffällig und gross," in NZZ *am Sonntag*, May 30, 2004.

Imprint

Editorial work Dominique Leutwyler, Zurich

Translation and proofreading Tradukas GbR

Graphic Design Bernet & Schönenberger, Zurich

Image processing Roger Bahcic, Zurich

Printing and binding Druckerei zu Altenburg DZA, Altenburg

© 2011 Verlag Scheidegger & Spiess AG, Zurich

© 2011 ProLitteris, Zurich for all works by Blanca Blarer (pp. 166, 168, 170/171, 172, 173, 174/175, 182/183, 185)

Verlag Scheidegger & Spiess AG

Niederdorfstrasse 54

CH-8001 Zurich

Switzerland

www.scheidegger-spiess.ch

ISBN 978-3-85881-718-1

German edition

ISBN 978-3-85881-253-7